636.800929

||||| |||| ||| || ||||| |||| |||| ||| |||||
D0452857

TYFOON'S TALE

The true story of a seafaring cat

By

SYLVIA MURPHY

First published in 2009 by
S.A. Greenland Imprint, 32 Morton Road,
Exmouth EX8 1BA, with River Media Group, Exmouth
www.rivermediagroup.co.uk

A catalogue reference for this book is available from the
British Library.
ISBN 978-0-9550512-3-4

Cover photograph by the author.

Printed in Great Britain by the MPG Books Group,
Bodmin and King's Lynn

DEDICATION

To all my shipmates, past and present, human and feline.

CONTENTS

PREFACE

I felt so sad setting off without a cat. Ships should have cats. Ships have had cats as members of their crews since time immemorial, and some of them have become quite famous, such as Trim, who circumnavigated the globe as the companion of Captain Matthew Flinders early in the nineteenth century; or Mrs Chippy, the carpenter's cat who joined Shackleton's Polar expedition aboard *Endurance*. The stories of both these cats' voyages show what a comfort a cat can be as a member of a crew, and how seriously they take their duties. They also show how seafaring cats can come to sticky ends but I ignored that side of the equation as we prepared for our great sea voyage.

Many people would have said we had enough to cope with without adding a cat to the manifest. The "we" whose sanity must be questioned in this case was two halves of a very newly married, very middle-aged couple, who were planning to spend their years of retirement cruising around the oceans on a ten metre yacht. To be precise, a sixty years old, ten metre long wooden yacht called *Nyala* that would have been welcome at a maritime version of the Antiques Roadshow.

The plan wasn't as crazy as it sounds. *Nyala* was, and probably still is, a beautiful boat, and we reckoned that if she had been floating for sixty years she would surely make it for another ten or so. I know that a floating home only ten metres long on an ocean the size of the Atlantic sounds disproportionately dangerous but a lot of people take on the challenge and come to no harm.

And a lot of them take their cats with them. I know, I've met them.

Our problem was that my faithful cat of twenty

years had recently died of a heart attack and it wasn't until the boat was ready and our route planned that I decided our ship should have a cat. David, the other half of the partnership, wasn't so sure, but then he was a less domesticated soul than I was. Ignoring his objections I contacted the nearest RSPCA shelter and asked if they had any kittens.

"Wrong time of year," they said. "You'll have to come back in the spring."

"I won't be here in the spring, we're setting sail before the end of the summer."

"Sail? You mean a boat?"

"A boat?" It was shock horror all round.

"You can't have a cat on a boat. It's a totally unsuitable environment."

I opened my mouth to argue, point out their error, then shut it again. Perhaps they were right. Suppose we took a cat and lost it, or it fell overboard and drowned? How would I feel then?

Terrible.

So, no cat. Catless we crossed the channel. Catless we cruised down the sunny west coast of France, around the Spanish Rias and headed for the south of Portugal, where we planned to spend the winter in a newly-built marina that was popular with small boat cruisers heading for the Canary Islands.

It was in the quaint, undeveloped fishing ports of Portugal that I began to notice something about the feline population that was beyond my previous experience. They were all alike. I mean, really alike, as though God had run out of ideas when he began to design their kittens. The Mediterranean tabby is a distinct type, different from the cobby tabby cats we are used to in northern climes, more like an off-shoot of the Siamese breed. They are small and slim with high haunches and long legs, and elongated necks. Their faces are pointed, their eyes and ears disproportionately large, and every one of them has an M mark above its forehead.

Years of unchecked breeding has resulted in a population of thousands and thousands of identical cats who live rough, nesting in pipes and holes in breakwaters. They are regarded as vermin by the local people, left at the mercy of little boys who throw stones at them, or grab the kittens when their mother is away and throw them into the harbour, laughing as the little mites struggle to swim. In fact, those are the least of the tortures they dream up. Charming though the Spanish and Portuguese are, there lurks beneath their civilised surface the need for adolescent males to prove their machismo through some act of cruel violence which as a matter of convenience is usually directed towards these ownerless cats.

The only people who give the cats any care are itinerant tourists and yachtsmen who might feed some of them and foot an occasional vet's bill but then they move on and the cats are left to fend for themselves again. Mostly they will scavenge from restaurant kitchens but there never seems to be enough food to go around and they end up with scrawny, diseased kittens, terrified of people.

Needless to say, my first instinct was to gather them all up and find somewhere safe for them but even in the wildest realms of fantasy it couldn't be done – there were simply too many of them. I later met an English girl who lived with her Spanish boyfriend in one of the towns we stopped in, and she had done just that. She ended up living in an apartment that was over-run with cats and their kittens, without the courage to have them neutered or return them to the outdoors. In the end her boyfriend gave her the "them or me" ultimatum and of course she chose the cats, which was a no-win situation because he was a Guardia officer (the equivalent to a policeman) and he was so put out by her rejection that he had her arrested and deported as an illegal immigrant. I never found out what he did with the remaining cats but I guess it wasn't pleasant.

Throughout that first summer afloat I managed to resist adopting one of these pathetic but unsuitable kittens. I didn't need reminding of the potential problems that would be caused by an animal covered with sores, bringing a huge flea population on board the boat that was our pride and joy. Further difficulties would include finding appropriate cat food (though these strays seemed to eat anything) and making suitable arrangements for the other end. It was one thing in the winter when the boats were moored to pontoons at the water's edge and animals could just hop ashore as though they were popping through a cat flap into an English back garden.

But most of the summer months were spent anchored in pretty bays where the only way to get ashore was by rowing in a small dinghy. I hear that chimpanzees have worked out how to do this for themselves, but we're talking cats here, and rowing isn't one of their usual skills. A shipboard cat needs a litter tray and I could see that it would never be easy to provide such a civilised amenity in a country that hasn't yet cottoned on to the idea of providing for the hygiene needs of humans, let alone cats.

Of course, my resolve didn't last for ever, otherwise I wouldn't be writing this book, would I? It was brought to an end one cold winter evening by an unpredictable combination of events.

1. FINDING TYFOON

Vilamoura, on the south coast of Portugal, was one of the earlier marina developments by the Portuguese in an attempt to provide safe amenities for the increasing numbers of yachts sailing south to the Canary Islands. It is an attractive place, consisting of a boatyard, a fishing harbour, marina pontoons with water and electricity, business and shop facilities and a range of modern apartments. There are hundreds of such developments around the coasts of Europe now, but in the 1980s it was a novelty and was proving popular with Portuguese families who could afford to buy a holiday apartment, as well as with the visiting yachts on a coast that provided little shelter from Atlantic storms.

At the time we arrived there the development was almost finished, but not quite. A couple of blocks of apartments awaited the attention of the gangs of craftsmen who moved slowly from one development to another. Because these caused dust as well as possibly adding a depressing air to the place, the yachts were being offered a very competitive rate per month for a long-term winter stay. After calling in to sample the facilities we decided to take advantage of this.

No doubt thinking it would be easier for us to

communicate with each other, the jolly Portuguee who ran the marina office had made the inspired decision to allocate berths along the pontoons on the basis of the nationality of each yacht. So there was a British pontoon, a French pontoon, a German pontoon, a Dutch pontoon, and so on. This did actually work very well. Manoeuvring many thousands of pounds' worth of yacht into a tight berth is no time to be learning how to say "Pass me your line!" in several different languages. It's better if you know you will be understood as you yell, "Get out of the **** way!"

To get back to cats – some time during our first week safely moored in the marina I passed a boat called *Tramontana* on the end of the British pontoon. Sitting on the deck in the sun, nursing three pretty kittens, was a mother tabby. They made such a charming picture that I stopped and involuntarily cried out, "Oh! Kittens!"

Almost immediately the Tramontanas' heads popped out of the hatchway. (We tended to call fellow yachts-persons by the name of their boat rather than the names they had been endowed with – it made them easier to remember. In the case of the owners of *Tramontana* everyone shortened this to Tramps, for obvious reasons). Mrs Tramp glared at me fiercely, as though she suspected I might try to kitten-nap her precious brood. "I'm sorry!" she said defensively. "They're all spoken for."

"*All* of them?"

"Yes. We're keeping one and the other two are going to our friends who have a farm a few miles away."

It seemed to be overdoing it to send two to the same home but I quickly realised, as I got to know Mrs Tramp better, that she had made these arrangements on the basis of only allowing her precious kittens to go to people she knew and trusted. It was to be many weeks before we achieved that status and by then the kittens had been dispersed and the mother cat taken to the vet in the nearby town to be spayed.

Inevitably the mutual interest in cats led to some socialising and before long I plucked up the courage to ask where they had found Peanut (the mother cat). She was another clone of the thousands of long-necked tabbies that wandered around the place. Had she been with them for long?

"We found her in the boatyard." Tears came to Mrs Tramp's eyes as she fondled Peanut's ears. "Last time we were hauled out to paint the bottom of the boat." (An uncomfortable necessity for every boat from time to time). "We'd been feeding some of the cats and one evening while they were eating, a pack of stray dogs came wandering around and one of them grabbed her in its jaws and ran off."

Stray dogs weren't quite as prevalent as stray cats, but they did make a nuisance of themselves, and even a scrawny cat must make a good meal for a starving dog.

"I'm not sure if the dog dropped her because we chased it with a broom or because she scratched its eyes but she was quite badly injured and we had to take her to the vet the next day. As well as patch her up, he said she was pregnant. So of course she had to come and live aboard to be nursed back to health."

So Peanut was one lucky cat – though not quite. She lived a life of luxury for several years on board *Tramontana*, cruising up and down the Portuguese and Spanish coasts, until one evening on the boatyard, in what was almost a repeat of her first encounter with the stray dogs, she didn't run fast enough. Perhaps she was slowing up in her middle age, or perhaps she had become over-confident. This time the dog that clamped its jaws around her tiny body made a better job of it and broke her back before he dropped her on the nearby beach where the Tramps found her. They rushed her to the vet but she was past saving.

But that part of the story was in the future on the cold October evening when we gathered for dinner with a group of yacht owners in one of the fine restaurants that fronted the marina. The ostensible reason for the dinner was to bid farewell to the two young Belgians who sailed on a small red yacht called *Tyfoon V* (note Belgian spelling). They had recently been caught out in mid-Atlantic by a horrendous storm that had all but broken their spirit, and they were flying back to Belgium the following day to spend some time deciding whether cruising was what they really wanted to do.

It had come as a surprise to David and me, novices at the cruising game, how cold it could get on autumn evenings after days of clear blue skies. This was made even more pronounced by the sea which in those regions was swept by the northerly Arctic current – what remains of the Gulf Stream after it has meandered around the northern ice shelves. The cold didn't worry us because our boat boasted a small solid fuel stove that would quickly raise the temperature in the cabin to a tolerable fug. Other, more modern boats were not so lucky and had to run their engines to keep warm.

It was late when the group split up in front of the restaurant to stagger our separate ways to our boats. We managed to find *Nyala* without falling into the water – not an easy feat on a narrow floating walkway, covered with a thin layer of ice, after a liberal sampling of the local wines. (This was where we learned about *Vinho Verde*). We slept well that night and in the morning, sitting on the deck drinking our coffee, we were surprised by the sight of the Tyfoons walking along the pontoon towards us, holding a pink towel very carefully.

"Can we come aboard?"

"Yes, of course. We thought you were leaving early."

"Yes. Our taxi to the airport will be here soon. But we have a problem here." And, almost apologetically, Mrs Tyfoon unwrapped a corner of the towel and out popped the head of a tiny, scrawny, dirty tabby kitten. Our eyes widened as the Tyfoons related their story in their charming broken English, each taking a sentence in turn in their rush to get it out in a way we would understand.

"We found it yesterday, after we left you. It was crawling around the pathway, crying."

"We could not leave it. It would soon have fallen into the water..."

"Or died of the cold..."

"We could not see a mother cat anywhere. So we took it to our boat and cuddled it all night but of course we cannot take it onto the plane with us."

"No. We brought it to *Tramontana* because we know she has kittens already..."

"But she said she has enough to cope with" – (this was before she had taken hers to the farm.)

"But she told us Nyalas are looking for a cat."

"And she gave us this..." A tin of cat food was produced out of a pocket.

"So you will look after it, won't you?"

We were startled and not initially totally enthusiastic. We had become used to being without a cat. We had a much better idea now than before we set off from England just how much trouble they could be on a boat.

"Well..."

"Oh good, we knew that you would." And the still-shivering pink towel was thrust towards us.

We had no choice. What could we do? We had to accept that *Nyala's* ship's cat had arrived.

And because the Tyfoons had brought her, we gave her their name. So, without meaning to, we took responsibility for a cat with the ridiculous name of Tyfoon.

The little animal really was almost at death's door. We offered it a saucer of the cat food that the Tramps had sent along, and some very diluted milk. It hoovered up the food in a matter of seconds, then lay in the sun, purring. It did try to keep its eyes open but its little head dropped forward and it slept for a while on the pink towel. On waking up it miaowed plaintively (it was more like a squeak really) until it was given another helping of food, when the whole process was repeated.

We took it in turns to keep an eye on the kitten, still quite sure that at any moment we would find it had died on us. But it didn't, and as that first day progressed it began to show an interest in a waggling finger. As the evening set in we moved it down into the saloon, pink towel and all, and made it a little nest on a shelf close to our stove. That prompted more fierce purring that seemed to last all night. The next morning food was first thing on the agenda, but this began to cause us considerable worry.

We weren't worried about where to buy further supplies of cat food – there was a well-stocked supermarket not half a mile away. What worried us was that the kitten had now assumed the shape of a tennis ball with a head and four legs sticking out, one at each corner. There seemed to be a real possibility that it would burst. I felt sure there must be something we could do to encourage the kitten's intestines to work properly - after all, if it had been me I would have taken a dose of Senakot but since the instructions with the packet forbade giving the tablets to children, I thought they would almost certainly do more harm than good and totally finish off the little refugee. So we cut down the food a little and waited...and waited. It took another twelve hours for anything to come out of her rear end. When it did it was to the accompaniment of squeaks and a bass line of rumbling squelches, and an unmistakable smell.

"You know," said David, "I think we'll have to provide a litter tray. I wonder how the Tramps manage."

It didn't take long to find out. We needed a plastic tray, which was easy enough to buy from one of the local shops, a bucket and a trowel. Twice a week Mr Tramp (later accompanied by David) would walk to the beach adjacent to the marina, noncholantly swinging an empty bucket, which would then he filled with sand. This kept the litter trays fresh. Disposing of the soiled contents was even easier – it would simply go over the side into the water. Mr Tramp had long since calculated that it would take about eleven and a half months for their boat to go aground on the discarded sand if they didn't move it in the meantime.

The Tramps also advised us to provide some grass for Tyfoon if we were going to take her cruising.

"Grass?" I imagined cultivating a small lawn on the afterdeck. "Are you sure?" Whatever did she need grass for if she had a perfectly good litter tray?

"Folic acid," Mrs Tramp said firmly. "They need it to keep their digestive systems in good order, and they get it from chewing grass. A small tuft will do. You can grow it on a plate, but be sure you keep it fresh."

She was quite right and Tyfoon loved her little patch of grass. Never mind the fact that either David or I would trip over it at least once a day so that it caused more bruised shins than smooth digestive systems.

It was obvious from Tyfoon's tabby markings, yellow eyes and elongated limbs that she had originated from the tribe of strays that wandered the area. Nobody objected to our adopting her because nobody wanted her, she belonged to nobody. But she must have had a mother and I couldn't help wondering what had happened to separate her from her siblings. I knew that in the great scheme of things it didn't really matter where she came from because it was obvious that she wasn't going back there. But how had she come to lose her family?

I came upon a clue. On her second or third day with us, when I was trying to clean up her still ragged fur, I found that one side of her face and one entire paw pad were covered with fresh scab tissue. Over the next couple of weeks it healed and fell off while Tyfoon was practising washing herself. I also saw that all the whiskers on the scarred side of her face were singed and it seemed obvious that she had been burned. But who would do a thing like that? And, if she was being burned, how had she managed to escape?

I mentioned this to Mrs Tramp who said, quite matter of factly, "It was the workmen."

"The workmen?"

"Yes, you know – that gang who were finishing off on the corner site. They had a big bonfire going a few days ago, burning the scrap wood. I heard them shouting and laughing as I was passing. I expect they found the kittens, probably the mother too, and threw them on the fire..."

"Would they...?" My reaction was as one would expect. Disbelief at first, then horror, rage.

"It's nothing to them. You know what they think of these strays."

"Yes, but...burning them?"

"Don't think about it," she said. Just be thankful

one of them got away."

If it seems that I drew extreme conclusions from the evidence of a few burns, that wasn't all. For the rest of her life Tyfoon hated the sound of male voices. Unless it was someone like David she had grown used to, she would run and hide at the sound of heavy steps and a deep laugh. For that reaction to persist for over eighteen years, the initial trauma must have been terrifying.

2. LEARNING TO BE A CAT

Contrary to what the RSPCA people had told us, the environment we had to offer seemed perfect for a cat, once we had provided the grass and the litter tray. She was too small to climb the companionway steps, so she could only go on deck with human supervision which meant that falling into the water was unlikely. If we wanted to go out all we had to do was leave her shut in down below, sleeping on one of the many nests of cushions we had provided ourselves with.

It never ceases to amaze how quickly cats learn. Okay, so you expect them to know about food bowls, and even to quickly discover what lovely stuff comes out of yogurt pots. Litter trays, yes, when their mothers are around. But on the very first day? And to find the cat-sized shelf above the solid fuel stove, first go – that's clever. Then to lay claim to it with the nearest noise to a thunderous purr that a tiny kitten can emit - that's miraculous. Almost as miraculous as the fact that when we finally put to sea and the environment began to rock back and forth in a sea-sick inducing movement, Tyfoon quickly found out that the centre of gravity, and therefore the point of least movement, was a particular spot on the cabin floor. There's no explaining it away as instinct.

It all seems to me as though cats must either think it all through, or enjoy some divine intervention in their learning processes.

The most important piece of learning, once she got a balance between her food and what was coming out the other end, was that she belonged with us on *Nyala*. By the way she took command it was clear that she understood we were her people and the boat was her home. Particularly the bit about who should sleep where. Again she discovered with uncanny speed that the warmest, safest place was stretched out between our two bodies, in the middle of the double bunk.

But why? She came from generations of strays whose only experience of human contact was bad, and yet she didn't seem to identify with them at all. She would watch them creeping up and down the pontoons and hiss at any who showed the slightest interest in coming aboard *Nyala*, so she knew they were there. But she was far more interested in accepting our rather soppy doting love and amusing us by playing ping-pong along the cabin floor, or inventing little jokes like grabbing discarded underpants and racing up and down the boat with them in her teeth, which would make us collapse with laughter. That takes a sense of humour as well as planning. When we had visitors for a meal and she saw the table being laid, she would sit in a spare place for all the world as though she knew we were going to serve food at any minute and believed she had been invited to join in.

As the weeks passed it became more and more obvious that Tyfoon had declared herself a member of *Nyala's* crew and had no intention of reverting to ordinary cat-hood.

The interior of a cruising yacht is a complicated environment. Everything fits together in the most spatially economic way possible so that there are few unaccounted spaces, and "furniture" is seldom moved from one place to another. This presents unexpected challenges to a young animal learning the twin skills of climbing and flying.

Did I say flying?

Nobody had told young Tyfoon that she wasn't supposed to fly, that it was a skill limited to members of the animal kingdom who had laboured over the generations to evolve the necessary apparatus. It simply seemed obvious to Tyfoon that if she wanted to get from one surface to another and there was a gap in between, she would take off and glide across the gap. It was an alarming sight and the fact that she usually made it was a triumph of optimism over the laws of physics.

A mile or so along the coast from the fancy new development of Vilamoura is the somewhat older and more haphazardly built town of Quarteira. We were first directed there by the Tramps, who were far too careful to spend their money in the shops that served the marina. While lacking any hint of architectural distinction it was – still is - a convenient place, enjoying all the facilities that the modern marina lacked, such as a farmers' market, a supermarket, a fish market, a Portuguese language teacher – and a veterinarian.

As soon as we were certain Tyfoon was going to live, and wanted to stay with us, we borrowed a wicker carrying basket from the Tramps and took her to the vet to get some jabs – particularly an anti-rabies jab which, we were told, was the normal procedure for pet animals on the continent. This seemed so logical that I fail to understand why the British authorities subject pets to the misery of quarantine rather than simply ensuring that they have been effectively vaccinated in their country of origin. It is well documented that the current system encourages owners who cannot face, or afford, the quarantine procedure, to smuggle unvaccinated pets into the country, which is far more likely to cause the disease to take hold.

The vet was a kindly young Portuguee who was anxious to establish a small animal practice where none had been before. Keeping animals as household pets was only slowly becoming accepted in modern Portuguese society so he was glad to have the custom of people like us and the Tramps, to lead the way by our example, so to speak. He pronounced our kitten healthy, sold us anti-flea and anti-worm remedies, and laughingly declared Tyfoon to be female. This was a surprise to us as we had been sure we had a male. "You should have realised," he said. "Such a smart cat could only be female."

He also told us that we must bring her back in three months' time for booster jabs and, later, for a spaying operation.

"Do you think that's necessary yet?" I asked.

His reply was firm and sensible. "This animal is not a toy, she is a breeding machine. Do you want to be acting as midwife on the high seas?"

I had only to close my eyes briefly to imagine half a dozen different horrific scenarios, every one of them ending with Tyfoon bleeding to death. They quickly demolished any further romantic notions about allowing her to have kittens and we pencilled into our diaries the date in March when, ideally, she should have the operation.

Meanwhile we were being mugged by the Christmas fiesta.

One of the things we had been looking forward to in our cruising life was freedom from the obligation to celebrate the ritualistic round of family festivals.

After all, how could we celebrate when we might be at sea on the relevant days, when we might be so far from civilisation that it was impossible to send cards or buy gifts? But on this, our first Christmas afloat, we were neither sailing nor deeply involved in other activities – except for bringing up Tyfoon, of course. And we really couldn't see how Tyfoon would be remotely interested.

Wrong!

Our first intention was to have a chicken for Christmas dinner, for just the two of us. But then we took pity on two of our neighbours who were singletons, specially when we discovered that one of them had an English Christmas pudding on board his boat – home made by some doting relative. So the party began to grow. We bought a plump, fresh turkey and all the trimmings from the farmers' market in Quarteira, though there was some communication difficulty over "sage". I couldn't see any hanging amongst the bundles of herbs on the vegetable stall and I just didn't have sufficient grasp of Portuguese to explain that what I wanted were the leaves of a small aromatic bush that would be chopped up and put inside the turkey. Mercifully I was rescued by an English lady who lived locally and translated my needs into *"salvia"* before the entire population of stallholders joined in.

I should mention here that Portuguese is a devilishly difficult language to learn – it looks like Spanish but is pronounced according to a completely different system. We were frequently frustrated by our teacher beseeching us to "run your words together! Run your words together!"

"Yes, yes. We know we must do that. But how can we when we have no idea what the next words are supposed to be?"

Anyway, back to Christmas. Tyfoon loved the

whole thing. She was so certain that something special was going on that she didn't sleep a wink for the whole of Christmas eve. She just laid down with one eye open when she felt tired. On Christmas day she became even more frantically excited at the sight of crackly red paper, the yards and yards of tinsel that one of our guests managed to produce from somewhere, and the smells of roasting turkey. When the time for carving the turkey finally arrived she waited her turn politely, though I think she must have found it very difficult to contain herself. When she was finally given a bowlful of turkey meat and chopped sausage she munched her way through it as though she was in heaven, then fell into a comatose sleep. And that's the way it has been for every Christmas of her life since. Except that last Christmas she didn't stop eating until she had demolished four bowls of turkey meat.

We were forced to take the vet's words seriously when Easter approached and the warmer weather began to beckon us out to sea (as well as the fact that the cheap winter berthing fees ended at Easter.) By this time Tyfoon was about half grown, a very pretty example of her breed, and beginning to take an interest in the outside world. Her favourite spot for keeping an eye on everyone on her pontoon was the bows of the boat. She would lounge there for hours, soaking up the admiration of passers-by. But so far, in spite of her flying skills, she had made no attempt to jump ashore.

Then the full moon waxed, and something extraordinary happened.

It was as though that first full moon in spring was a signal for all the stray cats in the immediate district to come on heat at the same time, and gather in groups to call. The sound was cacophonous. One cat calling for a mate can be disturbing and eerie, several dozen in harmony sounds like all the banshees from the underworld.

I thought that Tyfoon was obviously too small to join in this orgy, so we carefully closed all the entrances to the boat and went to bed as usual. The adult cats partied more or less all night, at least until the moon sank below the horizon, and the following day found a lot of bad-tempered, bleary-eyed adults, and no cats at all because they were all sleeping in their holes and nests.

The same thing happened the following night, with a rearrangement of groups and venues to provide variety. This time Tyfoon was keen to join in, and we thought not. Again we locked down the boat and went to bed, expecting Tyfoon to settle with us as usual. But Tyfoon had other ideas. Like a feline Dr Jekyll she changed from a complacent little innocent to a monstrous, raging bundle of fur and claws, bounding around the cabin, tearing at anything she thought might be a door or porthole fastening, or shredding our fine mahogany wherever she could see a gap in the hatches that could be widened, all the while howling and screaming.

She wanted to get out and join the party. She wanted to be a proper cat instead of the plaything of two elderly humans.

Sadly, but knowing she was too young to be properly on heat, we gave in to her and she sped out to join the group at the end of our pontoon. Whilst this was going on one of our fellow yachtsmen gave up on being tolerant at the prospect of a second night without sleep. He opened his hatch and yelled at the offending cats, at the same time chucking a bucket of water in their direction. They stopped their calling mid-aria, seemed to draw a collective breath, and scattered.

Tyfoon went with them, and didn't come back

the next morning.

It was easy to be pragmatic about the situation for the first day, to tell myself that she would soon find her way through the maze of boats and get back to us. Nevertheless, I felt very low at the thought that we might have lost our little cat for ever. Or even that we hadn't been good enough for her and she had deserted us. David may have been upset as well but he managed to hide his feelings and merely remarked, "For heaven's sake, she's a cat. She was put on this earth to have kittens, not to entertain two pathetic old fogies." Which was logical but did nothing to make me feel better, or to strengthen our relationship.

By the second day I could no longer contain my feelings and, miserable and weepy, I set out to look for Tyfoon.

It didn't take me long to realise the futility of looking for a small tabby cat in an environment frequented by hundreds of identical small tabby cats. Nevertheless, I persisted for the whole of that day, and the one that followed. I worked on the principle that Tyfoon might well be genuinely lost, as keen as I was to be reunited, and that hearing my voice would give her a chance to find her way back to *Nyala*.

But the only outcome of walking around, weeping and ostensibly talking to myself, was that a number of humans, and cats, took me for a mad woman and carefully avoided me.

Days passed, each as miserable as the last. My heart ached. I missed our little bundle of fur so much - I had obviously become far more attached to her than I had realised. The moon began to wane and the nightly cat parties stopped, but still there was no sign of Tyfoon. I began to wonder what we would do when the time came to be on our way at the end of the month. Would we simply depart and leave a gap in the pontoon for Tyfoon to find if she did eventually return? What else could we do? We could hardly leave her a message in the marina office.

Time dragged on, but in fact it was only a week later that we were woken in the middle of the night by a little whirlwind of fur and purring as Tyfoon hurled herself onto our bunk and began kneading at the duvet. It was obvious that she had been lost and looking for us, otherwise why was she so very pleased to have found us? She was desperately hungry and after wolfing down the best part of a tin of cat food she curled up between us and went to sleep. She had come home. Her first adventure was over.

3. LEARNING TO SWIM

Not surprisingly, Tyfoon had grown up a lot in that week. Mainly, she began to realise that she was a cat, not a human, and more and more she entertained herself with doing cat things. It was no longer a big deal for her to go ashore and to be seen chasing the Tramps' cats and blocking their trajectory so that it was inevitable that from time to time one of them hurtled into the water. That was a good game, and was yet another example of her sense of humour, her ability to think out cause and effect.

Now that she was beginning to socialise with other cats we began to wonder, not for the first time, whether it wouldn't be kinder to leave her to fend for herself amongst her own kind in Vilamoura instead of exposing her to all the scary and uncomfortable experiences we expected to meet as we progressed along the coast. It does make sense to ask why we were making this cruise at all if it was that scary and uncomfortable. The answer that came to my mind was that we knew what was ahead of us and therefore had a choice. On the other hand Tyfoon (and the Tramps' cats for that matter) knew nothing of what was to come and had no means of understanding that their happy life on the pontoon might soon come to an end.

The next few weeks were taken up with all the maintenance tasks necessary to keep our boat seaworthy. We watched other boats finish their preparations and depart, either for the Canary islands and an Atlantic crossing, or for Gibraltar and the Mediterranean, but we dawdled, unwilling to commit ourselves one way or another over Tyfoon. At least we were able to face up to having her spayed, though I nearly changed my mind when I saw her frightened little face inside the carrying basket as I deposited her with the veterinary nurse.

In Spain and Portugal they do a more drastic operation on female cats than we are accustomed to in England. In the past, when I had taken my English cats for the op they came back with a very small scar on each side of their body, where ovaries had been snipped out. Here, for some reason the vets do a complete hysterectomy which causes far more pain for the animal and takes longer to heal. However, Tyfoon knew nothing of these options or why we had allowed her to be carried off by a stranger in a motor car.

At the end of the day a still partially drugged Tyfoon was brought back to *Nyala,* accompanied by dire warnings from the vet not to let her walk about or climb for twenty four hours, because if she burst her stitches it would take about ten minutes for her to bleed to death. So we made a little bed for her on the cabin seat and were almost overwhelmed by the loud purring sound that is characteristic of cats in deep pain. Sometime during the night she did something that was fast becoming a recognisable characteristic of Tyfoon – she made up her own mind where she wanted to be and would brook no interference from me as she slowly and painfully crawled up the back of the upholstered seat, along her stove shelf and into the linen locker where she had the comfort of a pile of sheets and towels and the protection of a curtain. There she stayed, accepting small amounts of food and water, for the best part of a week, until it was time to take her back to the surgery to have her stitches removed. Being young and well nourished, she soon recovered from the surgery, but it took a lot longer for her to forgive me for sending her off to the vet. She made it clear that David was her favourite human by responding to his whistle when it was time for her to come in for a meal, but ignoring me if I tried to call her.

Cat ready, boat ready, weather beginning to settle into a high pressure pattern – it really was time to go. But go where? Our original plan had been to do the traditional route, sail south and catch the tradewinds and spend the following winter in the Caribbean. But David suggested it might be a good idea to try out Tyfoon's sea-legs (did he really mean Tyfoon's sea-legs and not his own?) by making the short trip to Gibraltar first. "We could just stick our heads into the Med, see what it's like, then go south. It'll only delay us for a couple of weeks."

It seemed like a good idea and it gave us time to postpone planning for what we would do with Tyfoon if she didn't like cruising. It's hard to believe, but at that juncture we were still prepared to find her an alternative, shore-based home.

In fact, to our enormous surprise, she loved it. Okay, she had some bad moments stretched out on the cabin floor, when her stomach was obviously threatening to part with its contents, but like any sea-faring human she soon got over that queasy feeling. That boring bit of sailing, to me, when the sea rushes past the boat in an endless procession of identical waves, was so exciting for her that she would sit on some unsteady-looking vantage point on the cabin top, just watching the movement of the water. On several occasions, schools of dolphins caused her eyes to nearly pop out of their sockets as she watched their antics with disbelief. She vented any spare energy by climbing the wooden mast and running back and forth along the booms, particularly at night, so that all we could see of her was something dark flashing across the arcs of the navigation lights. When we negotiated the entrances to the shallow rivers that are a characteristic of the southern Portuguese coast and dropped anchor for the night, she would accompany me in the rubber dinghy, sitting on my shoulders as I rowed ashore to collect fresh sand. Once the bucket of sand was aboard *Nyala* she would leap onto it and dig furiously, scattering at least half of it around the deck.

Along that coast, the first serious town we came to was Ayamonte, on the border between Portugal and Spain, situated at the mouth of a fast-flowing tidal river, the Guadiana. In the days before full EU membership, yachts used to be required to go into the harbour on the Portuguese side to check out of Portugal, then to cross over to the Spanish side to check in and buy a permit to travel up the river. There was no compulsion to explore the river, but it was a beautiful stretch of water, a recommended diversion amongst the yatchsmen who knew the area well. So one hot afternoon, beneath a deep blue sky with the breeze wafting the scents of almond blossom across the water, we picked a rising tide and managed to navigate up the river on the flood, meeting no one except the occasional group of fishermen with nets stretched across the river. They were none too pleased to see us, but polite with it as they quickly moved their precious nets and directed us towards the deeper side of the meandering river. Apart from a few small farms (including the one owned by the people who had adopted the *Tramps'* kittens) there was no habitation until, about twenty kilometres upstream, the twin villages of Alcoutim and Sanlucar faced each other across the river, one in Spain and the other in Portugal, with a deep anchorage in the middle pool.

It was a delightful place, quaint and quiet, except for the church bells, where one could experience the old Spain and talk to people who considered the greatest challenge in their lives was to cross the river illicitly and attend a party in the wrong country.

There we dropped anchor, unshipped the inflatable dinghy and rowed ashore to buy some groceries, and then settled down for one of those evenings that escapists like us usually only dream about – no electricity, no radio, no TV, no requirement to socialise with strangers. Just us and our books and our paraffin lamps, and the sound of the water trickling past our hull. Oh, and Tyfoon, who had invented a new game.

Darkness came early in those latitudes, even in early summer, and with it a variety of moths and insects that would have made David Attenborough proud, all attracted by the light that shone through our portholes. We had a net to cover the main hatchway so we didn't have to close ourselves in completely and, smiling indulgently at how sweet she was, we could hear Tyfoon dashing up and down the length of the deck, practising her flying, chasing insects. Happy? She was estatic.

We sat, we tidied, we wrote up our log, we read, we planned the next part of our voyage.

Then suddenly, both at the same moment, we noticed something . "It's gone quiet," said David as we exchanged glances.

Yes, it was quiet, too quiet. We could no longer hear the sound of a cat scampering up and down the deck above us. And we didn't know how long it had been before we had noticed it had stopped. All we knew was that she had gone, and we didn't have to wonder where.

"She's overboard!" I cried, grabbing the oars of the inflatable that bobbed alongside.

"No," said David. "She might be up the mast."

"Might be." He found a flashlight and shone it upwards but there didn't seem to be a cat, or anything else, practising gymnastics in the rigging. I knew for certain that she had gone into the river and been swept up tide, desperately struggling to keep herself afloat, probably squeaking for help from two people who weren't listening.

"She's gone!" David's voice broke a little. "We'll never find her now."

"We can't just leave her!"

"What do you want to do?"

The spring floods had left the river criss-crossed with small floating branches that regularly caught in the patches of reeds that grew in the shallows, making temporary islands. Tyfoon could easily have been swept into one of these and be clinging on.

Really? Did I really believe that? But I wasn't ready to give up. I climbed down into the inflatable dinghy, untied the painter and began to row, with the current, in the direction a small mammal would have been swept, all the while plaintively calling out her name, and listening for answering miaows in the darkness.

It was very dark indeed on that river and very lonely, but it never occurred to me that I might be in danger. All I could think of was how selfish we had been with the life of that poor little cat. How wrong we had been to bring her with us. She had been so happy in Vilamoura and we had imagined she would prefer to be with us and had thoughtlessly dragged her off on our boat and lost her, after only a week. And she had probably died in terror.

I hadn't gone very far on this hopeless search

before the tears were streaming down my face and a cloak of misery began to settle on my shoulders. How was it going to be on *Nyala* from now on, without little Tyfoon, who had so happily settled down as one of the crew?

I lifted the oars from the water and let the boat drift a little. The tide was turning and the current was slowing. I was still calling out Tyfoon's name and there was still no answer. Perhaps I should go back – what could I hope to achieve in this darkness?

Then I heard David's voice in the distance and I suddenly realised I had left him with no means of getting ashore and probably worried sick about where I had got to (well, I hoped he would be worried...) He was some distance away so it was difficult to understand what he was trying to tell me as he repeated his shout several times.

At last I picked it up. He was shouting, "Tyfoon! Tyfoon is here! Tyfoon is on the boat!"

I turned the dinghy and began to row back the way I had come. What a miracle! Tyfoon was on *Nyala!* How? Had I jumped to the wrong conclusion and set off to look for her when she was in fact hidden somewhere aboard?

When I saw her, a soaking bundle huddled in David's arms, it was obvious that she had been in the water, but how had she got out?

"I couldn't believe it," he said. "She suddenly came up the anchor chain about ten minutes after you'd gone. She may have been holding on to it all the time. We'll never know."

Once again, if only she could explain! That night we learned three things about Tyfoon. She was a strong swimmer, she could identify the hull of the boat from water level (and in the dark), and she could climb an anchor chain. We also vowed to worry less and trust her more but of course that was easier in theory than in practice.

That wasn't the last time she went for a swim. It became quite common for us to find a damp patch on the saloon cushions in the morning, or to hear a cat-sized plop during the day. Her preferred method of climbing aboard was up the balloon fenders – the soft plastic was something she could firmly dig her claws into. I wondered at the time why she had so many accidents until I realised that she found it very difficult to judge the jump from one moving object to another, so when there was a swell coming into our harbour and she wanted to explore other people's boats, she sometimes got into difficulties with her flying.

She never did become reconciled to actually enjoying a swim and she was firmly convinced that nobody else did either. Later that summer, when we had anchored *Nyala* in one of the Balearic calas, where it was possible to see the anchor chain snaking through fifteen metres of clear water and resting on the white sand below, I took to diving over the side and taking a few turns around the boat before breakfast. This horrified Tyfoon. She would rush to the edge of the deck, miaowing loudly, and follow my progress around the boat, never taking her wide yellow eyes off me. She must have thought I had fallen in. And again she showed her cleverness, reasoning that the water was just as dangerous and unpleasant for me as it was for her and I must be helped to get out of it.

4. LEARNING TO BE SHIP'S CAT

The Guadiana didn't seem quite so delightful after Tyfoon's adventure so we made our way down river to Ayamonte as soon as the tides allowed. Our next stop was to be Gibraltar. After an overnight passage (Tyfoon once again amusing herself by running along the boom and trying to climb the mast) we arrived just in time to see the magnificent sight of the sun rising over Europa Point and watch the arrival in Gibraltar bay of the long, lean speedboats that spend the hours of darkness smuggling English cigarettes to Spain and Morocco.

We moored at Sheppard's marina, a noisy cosmopolitan terminus full of boats of all nationalities, going in all directions, situated directly beneath the end of the airport runway. This location made it seem as though every plane that took off or landed was headed straight for us, which was scary as well as noisy. The only alternative was to use the anchorage on the far side of the runway, which we tried to do a few days later, only to discover that it was even more noisy and scary, with the added discomfort of bouncy waves when the wind blew into the bay.

In spite of all these disadvantages we liked Gibraltar – and that means all of us, Tyfoon included.

For a start, after the days we had spent on anchorages, she had a pontoon to play on once more. And there were other cats to visit. Some nervous owners bought little harnesses for their cats and fastened them to their boats. We did try this for a day but Tyfoon was quick to discover how to slip out of her harness. It wasn't that she wanted to go anywhere else. She just wasn't going to be told by us where she could and couldn't be.

As usual, advice came pouring across the water from people who were trying to be helpful.

"You shouldn't let her wander about. What if she falls into the water?" Well, we knew the answer to that one. She would swim around until she found a convenient fender and climb out.

"What if she meets up with a dog?" There were dogs on some of the boats and I rather thought that if there should be a confrontation the dog might be well advised to back down.

"What if she goes too far and gets lost amongst all these boats?" What, Tyfoon, not know where she was going or how to get back?

Of course, she came to no harm and we realised just how much we had come to trust her capabilities. It only slowly dawned on us that we still had a lot to learn about her, and the next lesson was that she was an opportunist second to none.

Moored near to us were the Fanciullas. Despite the Italian boat name they were an English couple we had met earlier in our cruise, in Western Portugal, and we had done them a favour when they lost an anchor. They invited us over for a meal one evening, cooked a roast chicken with all the trimmings and served it with lashings of cheap Portuguese wine. Tyfoon took no interest in this, preferring to spend the evening in the peace and quiet of *Nyala's* cabin. She was asleep there when David and I finally staggered back (without mishap) to our own bunk and settled down for the night. It was a hot evening so we didn't lock any of the hatches; the cabin was more comfortable with a breeze wafting through.

Aboard *Fanciulla* they thought the same, but also neglected to stow the remains of their chicken carcase in their cool box.

When they came to clear up their galley in the morning, the chicken was eaten down to the bone. At first each thought the other had woken in the early hours of the morning and had an extra snack – after all, the meal had been very tasty. Then as they discussed it they each remembered being half-awake and hearing a slurping noise coming from the galley. Closer examination of the chicken remains revealed rough rows of teeth and claw marks, and shreds of white flesh littering the floor. Somebody or something had definitely raided their galley.

The Fanciullas were unsure, unwilling to accuse Tyfoon when she hadn't actually been seen at the scene of the crime. Guided by the greasy paws and whiskers, and the occasional belch that came from the sleeping cat's stomach, we were far more ready to assume that Tyfoon was the culprit. But in the end, so what? If we had left her to fend for herself, she would have been totally reliant on the pickings from other people's galleys. It was comforting to know that she was capable of sussing out the closest source of food and making the most of it. After all, who knew what might happen in the future?

Mercifully our stay in Gibraltar came to end with no further cat disasters other than Tyfoon making herself very sick catching and eating a cicada that had made the mistake of trying to spend the evening inside our cabin. We left Gibraltar on the fourth of July and began to hop along the smart new marina ports of Andalucia, southern Spain. The first, Estepona, set a high standard for the rest as far as cat-kind was concerned. It had a stone pontoon, lined with beautifully cultivated beds of flowers – immediately given a good digging over by Tyfoon. On the boat next to us a kindly English lady whose husband had recently died, insisted on encouraging Tyfoon aboard her boat and feeding her the remains of the tin of salmon she had opened for her supper.

My log book also records that I made myself very popular by catching a large mullet.

Popular with whom? Who likes to eat mullet, especially around marinas where they feed on the detritus from the hulls of the boats?

Well, Tyfoon, of course.

One of the more useless pieces of equipment we carried on *Nyala* was a fishing rod. It was useless because neither of us was keen on fishing as a sport and neither of us much liked fish as a foodstuff. However, while we were passing the evenings on some of those Portuguese anchorages, I took out the rod and surprised myself by catching a fish or two.

"Ah, fish for supper!" I called, the first time I was successful. But David took one look at the creature neither of us could name, sitting in a bucket on the deck, opening and shutting its wide, ugly mouth in a threatening fashion, and refused to have anything to do with it.

Not so Tyfoon. She managed the extraordinary trick of standing with all four feet on the rim of the bucket and then leaning forward and trying to hook the fish out of the bucket with one forepaw. This was accompanied by furious miaowing and I got the message that she would rather like the fish for her tea. Once I had dispatched it and cooked it there was no doubt that fish was Tyfoon's favourite food and fishing her most favourite way of spending an afternoon.

How she knew this, without any prior experience, beats me. I can only assume there is some deep well of useful knowledge passed down in the memory banks of a species. If that is the case, she certainly had an ancestor who knew about fishing. She could recognise the sound of a line ratchet at a hundred paces and as soon as I put the baited hook in the water, whether on the boat or on a pontoon, she would jump onto my shoulders, peer over my head into the water, and all but point out which fat fish she wanted me to land.

In the hottest part of the summer we progressed along the undistinguished marinas of the concrete jungle that is the Costa del Sol. The only place we spent any time was in the old fishing port of Motril. My log book reminds me that this lovely old port was memorable for three things: firstly, we were able to take a bus from outside the port and visit that unmissable wonder of the world, the Alhambra Palace in Granada. Secondly, we took part in the Fiesta del Carmen del Mar (the feast of Our Lady of the Sea) when the fishermen brought their statue of the Virgin Mary from the church and took her out to sea to bless their fishing grounds. Lastly, Motril was the first port where we woke in the morning to find a guilty-looking cat busy washing herself in the middle of a very damp patch on the saloon cushion. She refused to say where she had been or how she had been so careless as to fall in.

By this stage of the cruise, going into a different port or marina every other day, I would have expected a cat to be pretty confused and fed up. I certainly was, because as we crept into each new port we never quite knew where to check in, or which part of the marina village would offer a launderette or a supermarket or a sensibly-priced restaurant. However, Tyfoon had it all sussed out. As we entered a new port she would position herself in the bows on the boat, sniffing the air until we passed the quay where the local fishing boats were unloading. I swear that when she located it she did a quick mental triangulation so that she would be able to find it again from the shore side. As soon as we were moored alongside our allocated berth she would be standing by the rail, ready to jump ashore. This may sound as though she was trying to escape from the boat but in fact she was simply full of joy at having a new place to explore. The Spanish are very good at laying out flowerbeds and shrubberies whenever they have built somewhere new and nothing threw Tyfoon into a greater paroxysm of excitement more than a *paseo* (pathway) laid out with bushes and an adjacent fish quay. I'm sure that after dark she visited many a fish quay and feasted on scraps left over from the filleting and gutting process.

And what did she do in those bushes? It seemed that mostly she hunted, small creatures like beetles, slow-worms, rodents, anything she could carry in her mouth, bring on board *Nyala* and deposit either on our table or on our bunk, preferably in the middle of the night. One time she made friends with a small rat and sneaked it on board without hurting it, presumably because she wanted to play with it. My first sight of it was when I drew back the curtain to get a towel out of the linen locker and saw Tyfoon and Ratty sitting opposite each other, warily watching each other. I had obviously disturbed a game of "chicken moves first" because a split second later the little rat turned and ran as only a creature can run that is being pursued by several times its weight of tooth and claw. Unerringly it slipped into the bilges through a grating in the floorboards that was too fine-spaced for Tyfoon to follow, and it spent the next few days living amongst the ballast. Every now and again it would poke its head out to see if Tyfoon was close by (a rather sweet little head topped by two large round ears). Because of her excellent sense of smell Tyfoon was usually well aware where Ratty was next going to appear and she would dive for the protruding head, though never quickly enough to catch it.

I suppose I should have been firm about buying a trap and getting rid of the stowaway, but there was something endearing about the little creature, with his large round ears and wiggly whiskers. The matter was resolved early one morning when I woke up to a series of unfamilar crashes and scrabbling noises coming from the galley and found Ratty helping himself to a hearty breakfast from the stone jar where we kept Tyfoon's solid snack biscuits. Somehow he had knocked the lid off and he was scooping out the snacks with busy little paws. Tyfoon was nowhere to be seen but it was very early, only just after dawn, and she had gone ashore to play with the wildlife.

Seeing a chance that would probably never come again, I surprised myself as well as Ratty with the speed I moved across the galley and took hold of his fine long tail. I hoped no one was watching as, clad in a flimsy cotton nightdress, I hurtled out of the companionway hatch, leapt onto the pontoon and ran its length, making the shelter of the marina flowerbeds before Ratty recovered his senses and attacked me. There I let the little creature go and watched him scuttling into the undergrowth. I hoped he would find somewhere safe to hide before Tyfoon returned from her night patrol.

By that time we were pretty laid back about

allowing Tyfoon to go ashore as and when she pleased. We did discuss the matter.

"One morning," said David, "We'll be ready to depart and she won't be there. What'll we do then?"

"We could wait for her."

"For how long? What if she never comes back?"

"Well, cats disappear sometimes in England."

Thankfully, in reality it was something we didn't have to face up to. Tyfoon was too canny for that. Wherever we were moored, however busy the port, she had to make time to explore and she was always home for breakfast, without fail.

5. PROMOTION TO CAPTAIN

"Are you t'ship's cat, then?"

It was a question often asked by the wit of the party as holiday-makers from more northern climes, staying in the big hotels that flanked the beaches, took a turn around the marina after supper. Tyfoon would be sitting upright on the after-deck, squinting into the evening sun, apparently ready to welcome any of them aboard should they wish to come.

Often the visitors would stop and discuss how sweet she looked, and then discuss our boat as well, as though we weren't sitting a few feet away listening to every word they said. I often wished I could have taught Tyfoon to say, "Ship's cat? No, I'm t'Captain."

Because, basically, that was the rank she had attained by the time that first summer came to an end. Or at least, it seemed like that, because every decision we made rested on whether it would meet with Tyfoon's approval, whether she would be safe, when for instance we went shopping or sightseeing, or whether she would be happy or not in the new place.

We had spent far too long in southern Spain, and the Balearics were so enticing that there seemed no reason to hurry to get to the Canary Islands. They would still be there next year. We had just made up our minds to stay in Ibiza for the winter when we received a telegram to say that my father, who lived in France, had been taken ill. As he was well into his eighties and this might be my last chance to see him, there was no question but that I should go, leaving David and Tyfoon to look after *Nyala*.

There were several ways to make the journey to St. Hilaire de Villefranche in the Charentes Maritimes where my father and his latest wife lived. That first time I flew from Ibiza to Barcelona and then caught a train to St Hilaire. On a later visit I caught a ferry from Ibiza to Sete, in southern France, and took a train from there. Either way, the journey was interesting, but as Tyfoon didn't come with me it doesn't fit into this story. However, there is something about that first trip to France that is about Tyfoon. I was away for about a week and when I returned I took a taxi back from the airport to the marina in Santa Eulalia.

I got there at about mid-day and David greeted me enthusiastically. "Where's Tyfoon?" I asked.

"Oh...she's here somewhere. She usually goes and sits at the marina entrance in the morning – I think she thinks she's waiting for you."

Suddenly there was a scrambling sound and Tyfoon's face appeared in one of the open portholes. When she saw me she began purring heavily. At the same time her eyes expressed some deep and satisfying emotion that was bubbling up in her little heart. After that she sat for the next couple of hours, her eyes glowing and the outer edges of her mouth composed into a smile, just watching me and listening to everything I said.

There is a school of thought that insists cats do not feel emotions. They say that we anthropomorphise our own feelings onto our animals and assume they are feeling as we do in a given situation. This seems to be a very narrow view. I don't think there was any doubt, that day I came back from my journey to France, that she was pleased to see me. I think it wouldn't be too outrageous to take it further and say that, by the nature of her response, Tyfoon was showing that she loved me.

We decided to ditch our long-standing winter plan of sailing south and crossing the Atlantic to the Caribbean. It was all very well thinking that a gypsy-like boat life would cut us off from the rest of the world and that family responsibilities could be ignored. The fact is that families are just as important however far away one travels, and often in need of support. While the trip to France reassured me that my father was not seriously ill, it also revealed that my stepmother was in the early stage of Alzheimer's Disease, which was driving my father crazy with frustration. I really thought he was going to murder her one day when he had to repeat to her for the tenth time what he planned for us to do in the afternoon.

In addition to that, my mother in England was showing signs of an illness that I thought was angina but which turned out, a couple of years later, to be cancer. And lastly, David was unwell. He began to lack energy and drive, his bones ached, he became impatient when things didn't go right. I tried to persuade him to fly to England for a few days and get a thorough physical check-up but he insisted he wasn't ill enough for that.

I didn't believe him. But he was a stubborn man and there was nothing I could do beyond nagging him, which I tried to do nicely. I could hardly pick him up and carry him to the airport.

We settled for spending the winter in the marina in Santa Eulalia. As with Vilamoura the previous year, because the building wasn't finished the winter mooring rate was cheap. The local people were friendly and welcoming. In spite of having several large up-market hotels, the town was quiet. It was the kind of resort favoured by the middle aged, and by the Spanish themselves. It had everything we could consider necessary for a pleasant stay - nice shops and small, family run supermarkets, a bookshop, an endless choice of good restaurants, a car hire firm, a yacht chandler, a launderette, easy bus connections to the rest of the island – and a veterinary clinic.

Why go anywhere else?

We needed the vet quite early on in our stay when Tyfoon took temporary leave of her common sense and tried to eat a wasp. When I saw what had happened I hurried round to the marina office and the very pleasant attendant directed me to the clinic, about a mile inland. There I found Martin Real, a large, jolly Spaniard, who administered the necessary anti-histamine injection and made an appointment for us to bring Tyfoon for her booster vaccinations immediately after Christmas. He completely dominated Tyfoon with his larger-than-life personality, which brooked no disputes and ensured that for the rest of her life she has never dared to argue with a vet.

The clinic was very convenient but it was inland, and therefore uphill, and Tyfoon was becoming a comparatively heavy, full-grown cat. A few days after my first visit I was trying to think of a way of carrying her up there, safe in her basket, without nearly breaking my back. As I passed a rubbish collection point out on the street my eye fell on a small, old-fashioned, child's folding pushchair. I wondered why it had been discarded. There was nothing wrong with it except that it had grown old and rusty – probably it had been used continuously by an increasing family and had finally become too tatty for their latest babe. I carried it back to *Nyala* and was delighted to find that the cat basket fitted neatly into the seat. Problem solved! For the rest of that winter I not only wheeled Tyfoon up and down the hill to the vet, I wheeled our laundry to the launderette, and also wheeled heavy items of shopping through the town. I must admit I had some very strange glances from Spanish matrons, specially when they saw that I was using the pushchair for a cat.

Not only did we settle happily in Santa Eulalia, Tyfoon thought it was a pretty good place as well. A wonderful variety of wild and cultivated vegetation surrounded the marina environs, making the almost daily offering of prey ever more varied. We never had another Ratty, but there was a steady supply of mice, and large caterpillars, probably those of the Elephant Hawk Moth, though identification wasn't infallible because we hadn't thought to bring a moth and butterfly book to sea with us.

The town and the marina had the usual colony of stray tabby cats (I'm told that this should be called a Comfort of cats) and at first we were concerned that Tyfoon, being a newcomer to the town, might be bullied by them. But not so. On the contrary, she seemed very successful at making friends. As the weeks progressed she singled out one identically marked tabby tom and brought him back to the boat every evening to share her supper. We nicknamed this cat "Hourigan" (Spanish for hurricane, which seemed to go well with Tyfoon). Hourigan never entirely trusted us, but was quite happy to raid the galley and biscuit jar in Tyfoon's company if we were out.

David and I also began to make friends as the winter set in. There were other English yachts in the marina, as well as a number of English people who had set up businesses in the town. As a result it was quite common for us to go to one of the many restaurants in the town for the usual sort of jolly evening that people enjoy everywhere, of socialising with good company over a bottle of wine and simple but well-cooked food.

I mention this because it soon became obvious that Tyfoon thought it was a pretty dangerous thing for us to do, disappearing into the busy town after dark, leaving her in charge of the boat. She took to following us out of the marina and watching which way we were going, then she would crouch in some dark corner until we came back, emerging to join us as soon as she heard our voices.

Shortly after Christmas we took advantage of the well equipped boatyard attached to the marina and had *Nyala* lifted out of the water for such annual maintenance tasks as scraping and painting, and checking sea-cocks. It meant spending a few days living propped up in the air with only a rather steep ladder to get in and out of the boat. As usual, we were worried about how Tyfoon would manage and we assumed she would stay on the boat – after all, cats are not renowned for being able to negotiate ladders. But Tyfoon never even considered it to be a problem. As soon as it was dark on our first evening in the yard, she launched herself head first, forwards down the ladder, spent a couple of hours exploring and playing in the yard, then came up again as though ladders had always been part of her life.

Unfortunately, the following day we were devastated to see that she was unwell, with increasingly severe diarrhoea and vomiting. I bundled her into her basket and hurried through the town to see the vet, who was becoming quite a friendly fixture in our lives. He confirmed my suspicions that she had been poisoned. It wasn't surprising that the Spanish boatyard crew would use some form of rat poisoning to keep the yard clear of vermin. Tyfoon had just been unfortunate during the few hours she had been exploring on her own, and had either eaten a poisoned rat or mouse, or picked up a piece of poisoned bait.

Martin, the vet, shook his head sadly. "I don't know if I can save her." But he tried. He gave her a hefty injection and instructed me to keep her cool and make sure she had plenty of water to drink. "She is young and strong," he murmured. "She may pull through."

Back in the boat she slept for what was left of the day but when it grew dark she insisted on dragging herself to her feet and making her way unsteadily down the ladder into the open air. I followed her with her drinking bowl and sat with her when she settled into a corner of the yard where she could watch the moon rising and the water lapping against the wall. She can't have been comfortable. She wouldn't lie down and she refused a series of cushions I fetched for her. I tried to hold her in my arms but she struggled free. She simply sat, staring ahead of her, and every time it seemed as though she was too exhausted to continue, and began to keel over to go to sleep, she jerked herself upright. It was as though she knew that if she gave in and closed her eyes, she would never open them again.

All through the night I sat there with her, wanting to hold her but unable to do anything but watch her struggle to stay alive. When morning came, she took a long drink of water, then dragged herself up the ladder, settled down in the saloon and went to sleep. We watched her anxiously, every moment expecting that she would stop breathing. But by evening she was ready to take a little food and the following day she was running around again as though nothing had happened.

But I was aware that something extraordinary had taken place. She had stared death in the face and decided she didn't want to go. She had fought against it with every sinew of her little being, and she had won.

By the time summer came round again and the cruising yachts were making their plans for the season, David's health reached the stage when I wasn't sure that he had the strength to manage a boat at sea. Yet, typically, he still refused to consult a doctor. Faced with the prospect of spending the whole long, hot summer in the marina, we thought it would be a good idea to rent one of the many little white houses that were scattered across the landscape of Ibiza. There David could paint and I could write and he believed he would recover his health. When he was well again we could move back onto the boat and continue with our cruising plans. We found a house quite easily, about a mile or so outside Santa Eulalia, owned by a widow who lived in Barcelona. (The distance from Santa Eulalia could be measured by the fact that I could buy a block of ice cream in the town, put it in the basket of the old bicycle I began to use, and get it back to the house before it started to melt.)

There was no question for either of us but that Tyfoon would come to the house with us, or that she would enjoy having a larger territory to explore that offered a far more congenial environment for a cat than a boat. She would make the most of the few months we planned to be in the house, then come back to *Nyala* with us and continue her sea-going career. We even decided to promote her to being "T'ship's captain".

So the very last thing we did on the day we moved our more important possessions ashore was put an uncertain Tyfoon into her basket and drive her up to the house in the old banger we had bought.

TYFOON'S TALE

We genuinely believed this was only a temporary arrangement. I didn't know that Tyfoon would never see her boat again.

6. LIVING ASHORE

Tyfoon hated the house.

She hated the wide open spaces, she hated the sounds and scents of the countryside, she hated the other cats who came to call.

But mostly she hated the fact that it wasn't her boat.

When we took her basket out of the car and carried it inside, she peered anxiously out through the bars. She showed some signs of eagerness to get out and explore as I undid the lock but as soon as she saw the wide tiled expanse of the Spanish living room, the walls further apart than anything she had experienced before, she spun round on her tail and dived back into the basket.

Bad idea, Mum. Let's go back home.

She didn't understand, of course, that this wasn't an option for the present. All she knew was that I didn't understand that living in this horrid new place wasn't to her liking. Not even when we made her a cosy bed and feeding station in a safe corner of one of the smaller rooms. She just sat, at first refusing to move from inside her basket. Later she crept out and curled up on her blanket and went to sleep, adopting what was to become her strategy for dealing with misery throughout the rest of her life – if in doubt, sleep; it may go away.

Fortunately she showed no inclination to try to find her way back to the boat, which had been my greatest worry. She could easily have disappeared for ever, wandering around in the unfamiliar countryside where packs of wild dogs roamed at liberty. Sensibly she left something as difficult as that for us to deal with.

The house, locally known as Can Vidal, had been empty for some months before we took over the tenancy, but we quickly discovered that at one time it must have been a haven for a sorry gang of cats. I call them sorry because they were not the Mediterranean tabbies we had seen in so many places along the coast. They were an assorted bunch of northern European varieties, ginger, tortoiseshell, black, white, and they had obviously been abandoned at one time or another by owners who had brought them to live here and then gone away. I understood this clearly on the day when a beautiful black tom cat wandered up onto the terrace and I said, "Hello, Blackie."

The cat turned and came across to me and purred. He had recognised the sound of his name, in English. I wondered what sad chain of events had brought him here and how long he had been fending for himself.

At first Tyfoon was intimidated by this gang as the word got around and they gathered on our terrace at feeding time. She would look at me as I dispensed the rations with an expression that said, "Do we have to live in this doss-house for cats?" But when I gave her a private feeding station on one of the kitchen worktops she began to feel more secure and she relented a little in her attitude to the whole situation.

The most senior cat in this gang was an enormous ginger tom who just had to be named Big Ginger. Like Blackie, he was habituated to humans and after he had eaten he would come into the house and fall asleep on the settee. One evening, when we had been in the house for about a fortnight, Ginger walked away, leaving his supper bowl only half emptied. I was about to chuck the remains, because if I didn't it would soon be covered with ants, when he returned, followed by a smallish white cat with tabby markings. He led her to the food he had left and waited while she tasted, and then began to gulp it down. Every time she paused for breath he placed a paw firmly on her head and pushed her face back into the food. As soon as she had finished eating she ran off but she came back the next evening, and the next, always following Big Ginger, and each evening spending a little longer looking around the house, as though she was preparing to move in.

It wasn't herself she was preparing for. A few days later I was sitting at the table in the living room, hemming a curtain, when I heard what I can only describe as several cats screeching at each other on the back terrace – a cat domestic, if you like. Hurrying to the scene, in case it was Tyfoon getting into trouble, I found one tiny ginger and white kitten, sitting on the doormat, crying very loudly.

"Ginger!" I cried. "What have you been up to now?" I was sure the kitten couldn't have found his way here alone, nor had he alone been making the noise I had just been listening to. This kitten must have something to do with Big Ginger and his little protegee, but where were they now? They had melted away into the fields and it was three days before either of them appeared again. By that time Little Ginger had established himself as one of the feeding gang and had almost decided that people were not as dangerous as his mother had led him to believe, though he hadn't yet reached the stage of submitting to being picked up. The little family was reunited on the terrace to thunderous purrs and a grooming session that threatened to strip the little fellow of his fur. We needed no further evidence that Big Ginger and his mate had planned this whole operation with a logic that cats are not supposed to possess. It reinforced that sneaking feeling that we had been manipulated by a superior intelligence.

Tyfoon kept her distance from the ginger family. Clearly she recognised that they were a unit that had nothing to do with her. Not so Blackie, where a tentative friendship began to form.

The busiest time for the cats was after supper (theirs and ours) when we would sit on the terrace overlooking the darkened valley, reading or talking, or sometimes just enjoying the cool air, and the cats would take advantage of the darkness to hunt the small creatures that inhabited the vegetation, bringing an occasional careless rat or mouse to be devoured on the terrace. When we heard the plaintive cry of an eagle owl hunting along the valley we would shiver with alarm, because eagle owls are huge birds that take rabbits, lambs and, of course, cats. But the cats heard them as well, and would rush out of the undergrowth to the shelter of the terrace where they would wait anxiously until the danger had passed.

On these evenings Tyfoon hung back at first, sticking close to us on the terrace. But, never short of a full ration of independence, she gradually grew more bold. It was noticeable that the cats (and by that time there were more than just the ginger family and Blackie and Tyfoon) preferred to head out on their hunting expeditions in pairs. And even more noticeable that Tyfoon and Blackie liked to team up together.

David and I watched this and wondered whether our precious little shipmate was in the process of becoming a feral and whether we would lose her there on that Spanish hillside.

"I hate to tell you this," David said one afternoon, coming in from the garden where he had started to build a wall around the edge of the terrace. His expression clearly said that whatever news he was about to impart would not be too upsetting.

"What?"

"I've just seen Blackie coming up through the woods, very slowly, stopping every so often to look back, as though he expected something to be following him."

Oh no, I thought. Not another intelligent cat organising a place for his offspring.

We waited expectantly that evening but nothing happened until the next day, when I heard the wailing sound of a cat in distress and saw Blackie approaching across what passed for a lawn in that dry climate, this time closely followed by a little black and white cat, who was the one making all the noise.

She was in a dreadful state. Not so much physically, though she couldn't bear to have her tail touched, as psychologically. Although she let me pick her up and cradle her, she was unable to go to sleep. Every time she tried to drop off she would start into wakefulness again, crying pitifully, and only begin to relax again when she saw that she was safe indoors with us. This went on for three days and I began to wonder if we had been picked up by the only insomniac cat in Europe.

Gradually she settled down and after being deflead and relieved of the worst infestation of intestinal worms I have ever seen, began to behave normally, with the exception that going out onto the terrace or into the garden was out of the question. Something awful had happened to her out there and I had a nasty feeling I knew what it was.

A large Italian family lived in the next house up the hill from us. As well as a tribe of assorted children, they had an even larger tribe of black and white cats. They were a wormy, half wild lot, never spayed or allowed into the house, and I guessed not actually loved very much. It was the sort of family where nobody would notice, let alone ask questions, if the children systematically tormented an animal, and I guess some of the little boys found it very amusing to tie up a cat by its tail and watch it struggle to free itself.

This cat didn't come with an obvious built-in name as the others had and after she had been with us a few days and it became obvious that she wasn't going to go away, David and I were faced with the question, "What are we going to call her?"

"Well," David said, half joking. "She's black and white like the Scotch whisky, so let's call her Scottie."

"No, no! We can't call a girl cat Scottie. It'll have to be Selina." So Selina she was, generally shortened to Selly. (For anybody too young to know, Black and White Scotch was a well-known brand at one time, though I can't remember seeing it for years; and Selina Scott was a glamorous television news presenter but she hasn't been around for a while either.)

One day, months later, the Italian father made a casual neighbourly visit to our house with some enquiry about garden plants, and he saw Selly curled up asleep on an armchair.

"Oh, that's my cat!" he said.

"No it's not. It lives here."

"You brought it with you?"

"Yes, and when we go we'll take her with us."

From the look in his eyes I could see he didn't believe me and I would be for ever branded a cat thief in that neighbourhood.

That first winter in Can Vidal sped by and the gang of stray cats grew steadily. Little Ginger metamorphised into a lovely, affectionate clown of a cat. He didn't stay little for very long because his favourite pastime was eating, for which he demonstrated an amazing capacity. Whereas all the other cats who visited the soup kitchen would stop eating when they had had enough, Little Ginger only stopped when there was nothing more to eat. After sausages his favourite food was spaghetti bolognese, which he would tackle by forming his mouth into a circle and sucking the strands of spaghetti straight into his stomach.

A little tabby tortoiseshell moved in, another sweet-natured animal who just seemed grateful to have a square meal once a day and, later in the winter, a place in front of the wood-burner that heated the living room. Fast running out of inventive names, we called her Tabitha.

Another tiny but very pregnant tabby and white mixture took temporary refuge under a chair on the terrace and proved to be the most intellectually challenged cat on the block. We were afraid she would have her kittens in the house but that didn't happen. Instead she appeared on the terrace one evening, her slimline stomach making it obvious that she had delivered her kittens somewhere in the last few hours. We thought she would eat and go straight back to them. But she sat on the terrace all that evening, and the following night, with a strange bewildered expression on her face.

The following morning she suddenly jumped up as though she had just remembered something important, and made her way down the garden and into the trees. I thought that the next thing would be her reappearance with one of her kittens. But after a few hours she returned, kittenless, still looking bewildered, and settled herself down under her favourite chair. She never did find her kittens – she had either forgotten where she had hidden them or they had been taken by some predator soon after birth. She wasn't a friendly soul so I was never able to catch her and take her to Martin the vet to be spayed, as I did with the others. I often wonder if she became any more competent at motherhood, but I fear not. She just had no idea what was going on.

Selly and Blackie became firm friends and I though for a while that Tyfoon would be miffed about this, but she didn't really mind. She was assuming a sort of leadership role in the gang, typified by her attitude to a pair of kittens we fostered for a couple of weeks for some friends in the town. As soon as they arrived she appointed herself official stepmother to the kittens and spent much of her time either watching their antics with a frown of disapproval, or washing them. One afternoon David and I were working in the garden, with the kittens and several cats, including Tyfoon, playing amongst the plants. Without warning a pack of dogs came over the hill behind us and, wisely, the cats scattered. All except for the kittens, who didn't know about dogs. They might not have survived, except that Tyfoon took charge of the situation. She stared at the dogs in horror, then looked at the kittens where they were playing nearby, then back at the dogs. Then she rushed over to the kittens and literally drove them towards a small pine tree and pushed them up its trunk, standing between them and the dogs until the kittens were safe, when she followed them up.

I thought that Tyfoon deserved a medal for her presence of mind. Not only had she proved once again her capacity to think, she had showed herself to be excellent mother material. What a pity she never had a chance to raise her own kittens.

7. DISASTER

As we passed our days pottering around Can Vidal, playing with cats and experimenting with growing vegetables, David became more relaxed, though his health didn't really improve. He tried to hide this from me so that I wouldn't nag him about seeking medical attention. He didn't even give in when I pointed out that our growing gang of stray cats got better care than he did. But to be fair, he didn't grumble about the vet's bills when I took first one, then another, to be spayed and vaccinated.

I began to feel the need to make a trip to England, partly to see my mother and partly to buy some new photographic equipment. I had always been interested in photography and with the fascinating twin subjects of the cats and the Spanish countryside, I was beginning to develop my skills, but I needed better filters and a more versatile lens. This need to touch base in England began as a little twitter of common sense (I could get this or that more cheaply in England, couldn't I?) and gradually developed into a sort of yearning (wouldn't it be nice to go shopping with my mother or sisters, like in the old days?) After some tense negotiation it was decided that I should spend a week in England, then return with my mother so that she could have a little holiday in the sun. The tension was because I couldn't resist trying, once more, to persuade David to come with me and see a doctor. But the harder I tried, the more he resisted.

There were all sorts of reasons.

"I don't feel well enough."

"That's what I mean. You should have a medical check-up."

"Who would look after the cats?"

"We have plenty of friends we could ask to do that." We'd already done the honours for some of them and had animal-sitting credits in hand.

"Tyfoon will be very upset if we both go away at the same time. She might run away."

Well yes, she might. But the chances were that she wouldn't. I said, "Are we going to organise the rest of our lives around one small tabby cat?"

"Isn't that what we've been doing? Why stop now?"

He was good natured about it, but intransigent. He simply didn't want to go to England. I tried to discover if it was my family that was putting him off (there are a lot of them and they can be noisy and intimidating) or the whole idea of getting into a airplane and taking two hours to make a journey that had taken us nearly two years by boat.

I gave up trying to persuade him. There is nothing worse than nagging constantly in the face of the other party's determination not to give in. But the uneasy feeling was growing that he was gradually withdrawing from being a sociable, outgoing person and trying to hide himself where nobody could get at him.

There must be something physically wrong with him, I told myself. Something like alzheimers, sclerosis, palsy – all those conditions began with some kind of mental withdrawal, didn't they? The truth was that I didn't know enough about neurological illnesses to be sure about any of it.

Of course, when the time came to depart I didn't want to go. I knew I would enjoy myself once I was in the midst of my family, but I couldn't stop myself worrying about David and Tyfoon, and I wasn't sure which of them I worried about most. David was obviously more important in my life, being not only a person but a husband-person. But Tyfoon was the more vulnerable, more likely to meet with something she couldn't cope with and so come to a sticky end – or so I thought.

My worrying wasn't alleviated by our not having a telephone in the house, so when I was away I couldn't phone David to reassure myself that he was all right. And he could only phone me from one of the bars or telephone shops in the town which wasn't always convenient. So I didn't expect a call every day. I'm sure that all sounds rather strange to anyone who belongs to the generation that thinks mobile phones have always been with us. Do you know that less than fifteen years ago there was no such thing as a personal mobile phone that you could carry about in your pocket?

Would it have made any difference to the outcome if we had been able to communicate by mobile at the time? It's a question I often ask myself and I'm not sure of the answer. When David collapsed he might have been able to summon help if he'd had a phone handy. As it was, he was left for three days, lying on the tiled floor, decomposing gently as the succession of evenings drew in and the cats gathered hopefully for their supper on the terrace. A supper – no, three suppers - that they didn't get, as a veil of misery, and probably panic, gradually descended on them with the realisation that once again they had been forgotten, abandoned.

Being the bright animals that they were, they tried to help themselves. Their first efforts were directed towards knocking over and emptying the rubbish bin, which yielded several tins to be licked clean and the remains of some bread and ham. But those didn't last long and so they reverted to their natural habits of hunting, bringing several half dead birds and rodents into the house to prevent them escaping before they could be consumed. Then, it seemed, they all piled into the double bed to pass the nights, perhaps hoping that one of us might reappear by morning.

Eventually a friend, concerned that David hadn't been seen in the town, drove up to the house and found him, or what was left of him, and events went into overdrive with an ambulance and police on the scene. The police would have liked to have had some witness statements, to make sure a crime hadn't been committed, but there was nobody but a row of anxious cats, sitting on the edge of the terrace wondering what was going to happen next, hoping for a meal but poised for flight in case the authorities decided to take them away.

The friend who had found David phoned me with news of what had happened. It was the day before I was booked to fly back with my elderly mother who was looking forward to her holiday. I remember taking the call and trying to make sense of the words that were coming through the phone.

"...too late to do anything...taken to the mortuary...a post mortem...."

I leaned on the wall, then slid helplessly to the floor, feeling as though something was exploding somewhere in the region of my heart. A procession of questions followed each other through my head. What's going to happen next? I'm a widow now, what must I do? How do I arrange a funeral? Should I try and get a flight back this evening? Who will help me to sort this out? It isn't fair. Why did this happen?

And lastly, though it may seem strange to relate that I even gave her a thought in the midst of all that panic, What's happened to Tyfoon?

I couldn't help it. Because once I knew that David was dead – and from the start of the drama nobody was telling me anything different – there wasn't any point in worrying any longer about what was going to happen to him. Caring, yes, but not worrying. So it was natural that I should compensate by worrying about what was happening to Tyfoon.

The journey back to Can Vidal was terrible. I couldn't eat, I couldn't stop crying, and my poor mother was trying to comfort me and explain to people what had happened. We had no idea what sort of state we would find the house in. But thanks to the efforts of my friends, when we finally arrived the place was clean and sweet smelling. Better still, the roll-call of cats was complete as they sat on the terrace, waiting for the next phase of our lives to begin.

It was pretty confusing at first.

It was some days before the coroner issued papers that confirmed what everyone thought – that David had collapsed with a massive heart attack. An attack that had been lurking within him for months as his clogged blood vessels and dirty lungs struggled to keep his blood oxygenated. What he needed, and had been so afraid of finding out about, was a quadruple by-pass.

There was no facility on the island for cremation – I would have had to fly David's coffin to Barcelona for that – so he was laid to rest in the municipal cemetery. This was a traditional Spanish burial ground, where the coffins were stacked in purpose-built high white walls, fronted by niches which commemorated the life and death of the occupant in the same way as a gravestone does in an English churchyard. This particular cemetery was in the most beautiful location that anyone could wish for, perched on the top of a pine-clad hill overlooking the distant blue Mediterranean.

After the funeral, and after my mother's visit came to an end, there was a stream of well-meaning visitors, all of them convinced that I shouldn't be left on my own. But being left alone to wrap myself in my grief was just what I craved. I was trying to take my mind off the situation by working on a couple of journalistic contracts I had in hand, the most important being a book about our boat *Nyala*. At the same time I had to wrestle with even bigger, whole life problems, such as whether I was going to stay in Can Vidal, go back to living aboard *Nyala*, or return to England and take up the threads of my previous life before I had met David.

The prospect of staying at Can Vidal was enticing. It was a beautiful place and I didn't mind the isolation, specially when I knew I would never come home to an empty house or sleep in an empty bed. Tyfoon was always waiting for me, snoozing in some sunny spot, and I would see her head raised as she heard the car labouring round the last corner on the road. I suppose initially when she heard that engine she thought it would be David coming home at last. She must have missed his presence in the house. It was he who had taken most time to play endless games of ping-pong football with her, or trail pieces of knotted string for her to chase. But I suppose she gradually got used to the idea that it was I who appeared when the car drew up, and I who fed her and combed her and made room for her on the bed during the long lonely nights. David's memory would have faded for her as well as for me, though I like to think that I grieved the longer. But how can I be sure?

I had a lot of adjustments to make. I was still responsible for *Nyala* but there was no way I could manage her by myself. It became obvious that even if I wanted to I couldn't go back to live in England while I had the boat in Ibiza, so with a heavy heart I had her hauled out of the water into the boatyard and put her up for sale. Once she was out of the way I would have one less complication to sway my judgement.

As time went by and I began to get used my grief I yearned more and more to be back in England. People thought I was crazy to want to leave Ibiza but in England I would once more have ready access to a market for my writing and photographs. My large family and circle of friends were just waiting to take me over and support me. In Ibiza I had no future but to join a circle of ageing ex-patriate widows squabbling over the local toy-boys.

But apart from *Nyala* there was one other thing, one very important matter, that stopped me packing up and going back. What was I going to do about Tyfoon?

I couldn't let her become just another abandoned cat on a Spanish hillside.

Yet I had to face up to the very reason why there were so many abandoned animals. They couldn't be taken back to the UK without spending six months in anti-rabies quarantine, and those six months, plus transport costs, would cost over a thousand pounds. In common with many pet owners I would have swallowed hard and paid out the money had it not been for the awful thought of what six months in grim and inexplicable captivity would mean to those little animals. Stories circulated about animals who had died in quarantine, many of them simply through a broken heart. There were stories too about animals lost in transit by the airlines and never tracked down again.

I just couldn't summon up the strength of mind to subject Tyfoon to any of that.

There was one glimmer of light. Several newspapers were beginning to report that the British Government was relenting in its harsh quarantine policy, mainly because with the new Channel Tunnel it was becoming impossible to enforce. The only cases of rabies that had broken out in the last few years had been in dogs smuggled into the country by their owners, or in bats that had flown through the tunnel and settled in Kent. There were rumours that the law was to be amended so that animals that had been vaccinated against rabies in their country of origin, and carried a valid certificate to say so, could be brought straight into the country at a limited number of designated ports.

That seemed like a sensible system. But vested interests, in the form of the profitable quarantine kennels, fought the legislation and delayed its implementation. So I stayed on, believing that within a few months everything would change and I would be able to get onto an airplane with Tyfoon in a basket beside me and take her home.

Time passed, and passed, and passed, and nothing happened. Winter became spring and my bank balance began to teeter. Rents were high on those beautiful Balearic hillsides, but I managed to get a seasonal job working for one of the local fashion houses, compering fashion shows for tourists in English and French. It was interesting, and fun, but as one year became two, and threatened to become three, I began to lose sight of my objective. What I really wanted was to go home to England, and I wanted to take Tyfoon with me.

8. QUARANTINE

It took an enormous effort to reach the decision that I had no choice but to send Tyfoon through quarantine. But it didn't stop at that. Was I going to take Tyfoon and leave Blackie and Selly and the sweet little Tabitha to return to their feral state? I calculated that by cashing in a life insurance policy I could afford the quarantine bills for four cats. Those four cats had to be Tyfoon, Selly, Blackie and little Tabitha.

I would somehow have made the money stretch to include Little Ginger and his mother but tragically Little Ginger had disappeared some months earlier. I never knew what had happened to him, though I searched like a maniac for days. I suspect that he fell victim to the eagle owl because when he played out on moonlit evenings his white bib would glow like a florescent jacket, making him the most conspicuous animal on the hillside. I dithered over taking his parents but as they were such an experienced part of the local cat scene I was sure they would be able to fend for themselves, though I did make arrangements for them to be fed by friends after I had gone.

Years later, when I returned to Ibiza for a visit and called in at Can Vidal, Mrs Ginger was still there, relaxing in the sun, though the occupiers of the house at that time were German people and they had called her Catz. They knew nothing of Big Ginger, had never seen a cat fitting his description. Even before I left Can Vidal I knew that he had been on his way out; he had been the victim of cat flu, then of a serious mugging that almost cost him an eye. Knowing that he hadn't made it, I felt guilty at having left him behind. But of all the cats that lived semi-wild on that hillside, I think six months in quarantine would have driven him to a miserable, heartbroken death.

Interestingly, one "new" cat I saw on that final visit to Can Vidal was a slender young black cat with a little wisp of white fur on his chest – the image of Blackie. It wasn't possible that this was Blackie's son – too much time had elapsed since I had taken Blackie away – but he was obviously from Blackie's gene pool. I rather like the idea that the gentle black giant had quietly fathered a tribe of beautiful black clones while nobody was looking.

Once I had made my decisions about who was to stay behind and who would come back to England with me, it took even more of an effort to start pouring money into the cat-sized hole I had made in my life.

The operation began with a few phone calls to a government office in London which resulted, pretty efficiently I thought, in an envelope full of information about where I would find out about quarantine kennels and catteries, and how to book a place in one. It also recommended that before making a booking, the pet owner should personally inspect the establishment, because the fact that they were on a list recommended by the Government did not constitute a guarantee of quality.

Good idea, I thought, thankful that I was only a two hour flight away from England, not trying to import

Tyfoon from the antipodes or the South Pacific. My inspection did nothing to cheer me up when I discovered that all the catteries on the list managed to achieve a similar level of depressing concrete surroundings – I learned that the concrete was so that the cages and their immediate environment could be effectively disinfected. They were all occupied by sad-looking cats, who cast anxious eyes towards the door when they heard footsteps approaching, hoping that, at last, *their* people were coming to take them home.

The cattery I finally chose had the advantage of being near to the West of England, but that was all it had to recommend it over the others. The fierce-looking lady owner explained that my cat(s) would be met at Gatwick by the animal handling department, and picked up later in the same day by one of her employees in a van that would transport them to the cattery. There they would be inspected by a veterinary officer and given a fresh set of vaccinations. I wouldn't be allowed to handle or visit them for two weeks after their arrival.

"How many cats did you say you would be bringing?" she asked me, her pen poised over an application form. I hadn't said, because my mother had come along for the inspection and I was anxious not to let her know how weak-minded I was being.

"Four," I muttered quietly, ignoring the gasp of disapproval from my right.

"And what date will you be sending them over?"

This was crucial, because from that date I had exactly six months to pack up my home at Can Vidal, bring *Nyala*, still unsold, back to England, and find myself a cat-friendly home in the South West. With growing sense of panic I named a date and the cattery lady smiled and gave me the necessary documentation in exchange for a lot of my money.

Back in Ibiza I realised I had very little idea how to organise four cats to fly to Gatwick. A phone call to the airline produced the information that the animals must travel as freight in the aircraft's hold, in secure cages. No, even if I was travelling with them, they would not be allowed in the passenger cabin because of the risk of injury to other passengers if there was an emergency landing. They had to be booked in well in advance and I should contact the airline's official local freight agent to make the necessary arrangements.

Cages? Air freight? Emergency landings? What had I let my poor furry darlings in for? Was it too late to cancel the flight and put them on board *Nyala* and sail them home? Surely nobody would notice if I arrived in Falmouth with a boat full of cats? But what if they did notice? What if the cats were summarily removed by white-coated men of the kind who visited farms during the BSE and tuberculosis epidemics, taken away and executed, and all because I had been too weak-minded to provide for them properly?

Anyway, by that time I had also received the pilotage information about the French Canals. Although it seemed like an easy option to sail to the South of France and navigate the canals, the trip was full of hazards like locks, river crossings, barges, sluice gates, unregulated overnight moorings. In a fresh outbreak of panic I quickly convinced myself that I would be lucky to get the boat to Falmouth without killing myself and my volunteer crew, let alone without losing four cats.

The airline's freight agent was an enormous and friendly Dutchman who met me in one of the local bars, equipped with a rucksack containing sheaves of official documents, and a small portable typewriter. He set up his mini-office on one of the bar tables and proceeded to type up the tickets and permits I would need in order to get my live cargo onto one of his company's charter flights. Despite his cheerful exterior and his reassurances that the airline carried pets almost every week, nothing he said made me feel any better about what I was doing.

"Now," he said, "You know that because of summer schedules this flight leaves at two in the morning."

No, I didn't know. I must have turned very pale because his expression changed from cheerful to anxious.

"You must have the animals at the airport two hours beforehand, all paperwork in order. You can manage that?"

"Yes, of course. What do I do with them when I arrive at the airport?"

"Well, don't try to check them in to the baggage. I will be there to meet you and I will personally see that they are put aboard the plane and properly stowed."

Wouldn't they be very frightened, boxed up in the hold, as the plane took off? It was bad enough being a human passenger during takeoff, knowing what was happening and why. Being a small captive animal was surely enough to cause a heart attack?

"Should I give them a sedative before they travel?" I asked him.

"That's up to you, but I don't advise it. Some people have given them too much and they haven't woken up again. Why don't you consult your vet?"

Martin the vet, who by that time I knew pretty well, also advised against it. He laughed in his usual jolly, heartless way. "They'll be all right," he said. "They'll shout a bit at first then they'll just lie down and sleep until it's all over."

How did he know?

I had a week to finish the preparations for the cats' departure. I bought their travelling cages at the local pet shop and I tried to prepare them for their ordeal by putting them into the cages every evening and taking them for a short car ride. I don't know if it helped but at the time I believed it would give them confidence.

Then the great day arrived. They had their final check-up at the vet and after their supper I eased them inside the house and made sure all the doors and windows were closed. Anyone who has been faced with the problem of rounding up one cat to put into a carrying cage will understand exactly how difficult it was to make sure I had four of them in the right place at the right time. Somehow I managed it and was finally buzzing along the road to the airport in the heavy Spanish dusk trying to ignore the occasional wail of protest telling me that we had gone far enough, we hadn't been this long on our previous car rides, did I know where I was going?

I arrived at the little airport at about the same time as the incoming charter flight was disgorging its package holiday passengers. By chance I found a group of friends waiting to see off some visitors and they helped me carry the caged cats into the busy concourse. Seeing how the milling people and bright lights caused the cats to cower into the back of their cages, I was almost ready to give up the whole project and drive them back to Can Vidal and stay there with them for ever. But then the Dutchman arrived and took over and everything was out of my hands. I had only to go and sit in the bar chatting with my friends until he found me and told me my animals were safely aboard, he had personally stowed and fastened their cages, and the next thing I would hear would be a message from the cattery driver in the morning to say that he had picked them up safely.

I stayed at the airport until I could watch the plane

taking off, all the while imagining little hearts beating with terror. Then it was time to go back to Can Vidal and sit on the terrace with Big Ginger, watching the sunrise and trying to explain to him where the gang had gone.

It would be nice to be able to conclude this chapter by saying that everything went according to plan, but it didn't. Later that morning I was drinking coffee with a sympathetic friend who had dropped in to make sure I was surviving the trauma of finding myself in an almost catless house. I wasn't alarmed when the phone rang (by that time I had a phone connected to the house) and I wasn't alarmed when voice said, "Mrs G? This is Tom from the South West Cattery." This would be the message telling me he had picked up the cats and they were on their way .

"Yes?"

"Mrs G, didn't you send your cats?"

"What?" My heart was thudding fit to burst as I lowered myself onto a chair. "What are you saying?"

"I've just arrived at the animal holding centre at the airport and your cats haven't arrived."

"But that's impossible! I saw them onto the plane last night. They couldn't have got off by themselves. Are you sure...are you sure you've met the right plane." What had happened? Had they been stolen, diverted onto a flight to China to be made into trims for hoodies' anoraks?

"Whatever plane they came in on they would have been brought to the animal holding centre." Then, getting the message that I was very close to having hysterics, he said he would enquire further and ring me back. As soon as he was off the phone I got in touch with the flying Dutchman who, apparently knowing exactly where to apply pressure, had people turning Gatwick

Airport upside down within minutes. Still, another two hours passed before the cats were found, stacked in a corner of one of the baggage reclaim halls.

It appeared that some dozy baggage handler had unloaded them from the plane, ignored the bright red labels on their cages which said "RABIES CONTROL", and put them onto the baggage carousel where any of the passengers could have picked them up and taken them away. Someone had then taken them off the carousel and, not knowing what to do with them, parked them in a public concourse. By the time they were found they had been sitting there for hours, thirsty, dirty and distressed.

I was assured that they had come to no harm but it was difficult not to think about all the awful things that might have happened to them. They spent the night free of charge (I should think so!) at the animal centre and were picked up by the cattery driver the next day.

I don't know whether I was relieved or heartbroken to know that their fate was now out of my control. My mother tried to visit them at the cattery to make sure they were all right but she was firmly turned away – it was too soon. I wouldn't be able to see them until I had negotiated around a thousand miles of canals and seaway, so I had no choice but to get on with it.

9. BURNGULLOW

It took me all of six weeks to pack up at Can Vidal and bring *Nyala* back to England via the French Canals and the Bay of Biscay. As I sailed away from Santa Eulalia with my sister and her husband as crew I felt choked with sorrow at having to leave Can Vidal with its friendly thyme covered hillside. But once Tyfoon and the gang of strays had gone, the house began to lose its spirit.

The voyage home was another adventure, starting with a storm off Barcelona. That immediately convinced me that I had been right to exclude the ship's cat from this experience. Tyfoon wouldn't have enjoyed the rough sea, the thunder and lightening. Nor would she have enjoyed the masts being lowered and stowed for the canal trip. As for going through locks, with their rushing waters and high, mossy walls – they terrified me and I understood what they were all for. If Tyfoon had fallen in the water in a lock she wouldn't have been able to climb out and would either have been crushed between the boat and the wall, or sucked through one of the sluices. I soon convinced myself that, however traumatic the plane ride and however depressing the quarantine cattery, Tyfoon had the best of it that summer.

I knew that my mother was fretting because it

seemed to take for ever to get *Nyala* back to England but there was nothing I could do about it. We came as quickly as we could but sailing a boat is very little faster than walking and there was a long way to go. The part of the journey that took us through the Canal du Midi had a charm all of its own, wending its way through regions that I had only previously read about on the labels of wine bottles. The Canal Lateral that took us into the Garonne River and thus into the Bay of Biscay, was more difficult, fraught with dangers such as huge barges that threatened unceremoniously to run us down if we didn't get out of their way. The final reaches of the Garonne, leading us through the Gironde Estuary were shrouded in fog and plagued by fierce tides.

Finally, one hot afternoon in July, it was all over. Six years and 3500 miles after we sailed out of Falmouth, catless, I returned with a fully trained ship's cat and auxiliary feline crew. A pity the picture was spoiled by the fact that Tyfoon and her gang were still incarcerated in the quarantine cattery.

The day after our arrival I was driving along the A30 from Falmouth towards the cattery to make my first visit. I was very nearly choking with a mixture of excitement and trepidation, wondering what I would find. Would they be terribly depressed and unhappy? Would they expect me to rescue them immediately? Would they ever forgive me for what I had done to them? Would Tyfoon even remember me ?

Their reactions were all different. As soon as

I appeared in their enclosure Blackie stuck his nose in the air and stalked through their access door to the outside part of the cage he shared with Selly, where he sat for the whole of the rest of my visit facing the wall, refusing to look at me. Selly and Tabitha were delighted to see me, played with the toys I had brought them, and didn't consider any punishment necessary. Tyfoon clearly didn't want me to touch her; she had perfected an eloquent trick of walking away from me sideways, so that she proscribed a circle with her eyes averted, yet at the same time somehow never left my side. When the visit was over and I looked for Tyfoon to say goodbye I couldn't see her anywhere. Then I found that she had sneaked into the grip bag that I had left standing on the floor near the door.

I didn't kid myself that she had done that because she was fond of me and wanted to stay with me. Nor could I say with certainty that she knew that it might be the most successful ploy to regain her freedom. But it rather looked as though, once again, she had applied some logic to the situation. It certainly upset her, and nearly broke my heart, when I had to extract her from the bag and leave her behind.

I visited several more times during the next few weeks, but not as often as I might have done, because I found it such a depressing experience and I was sure the cats also found it upsetting. I suppose I might have felt better if I had been able to explain to them what was happening, perhaps make them a kind of advent calendar to tape onto their wall. When I thought of that I suspected that I was beginning to lose my grip on the situation. What was the point of giving them a calendar if none of them could read?

At the same time I was dashing around the

countryside on the Devon/Cornwall border looking for a cat-friendly home. I suppose I was hoping to find something that reminded me of Can Vidal because if it reminded me, it would remind the cats. Eventually I settled for a dilapidated bungalow on the edge of a Cornish village, surrounded by open fields with a stunning view across thirty miles of landscape. It was in china clay country, in a corner known as Burngullow, which I later learned meant Sunny Hillside in the Cornish language.

In the end, what with the usual legal requirements for purchasing a property, there wasn't much time to spare. I managed to sell *Nyala*, complete the necessary negotiations to buy the bungalow, and move in with the household possessions I had shipped back from Spain, only a few days before the end of the quarantine period. I did everything I could to ensure the cats would like their new home – I bought new feeding bowls and litter trays, blankets and beds. I fitted a series of cat flaps in the back porch. With hindsight I should have sent warning notices around to the local wildlife.

As I set off on the last run out to the cattery I realised that I had managed to achieve something that had seemed impossible nearly a year ago. I had brought Tyfoon and her gang safely back to England, where I would be able to care for them for the rest of their lives.

When I arrived back at the bungalow on that momentous day, I let them out of their carrying containers in the living room and just sat and watched them, wondering how they would react. Eagerly they sniffed around, trying to identify which bits of furnishings were familiar and which were strange to them. Tyfoon was particularly interested in the Persian rugs that had been on the floor at Can Vidal and after she had identified them she did something I have never seen a cat do, before or since. She put her head down onto the rug and turned a series of somersaults.

I thought it fair to interpret that as pleased to be home.

They all expressed their excitement in some individual way. Selly went straight out into the garden and caught what must have been the only careless lizard in Cornwall. Blackie took off on long expeditions down to the nearby china clay works – I thought I had lost him the first time he did this but he returned safely the next morning, all four paws clogged with tell-tale white mud. Tabitha quickly found the sunniest places to sit and watch the world go by. And Tyfoon?

Tyfoon treated the bungalow as though it was a boat. Every evening she accessed the roof by climbing the posts that held up the creeper-covered pergola in the garden, and spent hours running up and down the pitched slopes. Her scampering feet overhead reminded me of the evenings when she used to chase moths and insects up and down *Nyala's* deck. But she never fell off the roof. No doubt she was relieved to find a place that had all the friendly characteristics of her one-time boat but none of that dangerous water stuff around it.

"Come on, who's coming for a walk.?" More the sort of thing you'd expect to hear a dog being asked, but I never did explain this fine distinction of expectation to Tyfoon. She wouldn't have taken any notice of it anyway – Tyfoon did what she wanted to, not what a cat was expected to do.

Our afternoon walks consisted of circling the inner hedgerows of the fields adjacent to our bungalow, and there were all kinds of interesting smells to be investigated on the way. There was one particular gap in the hedge where a little path ran through the thick undergrowth and across the next field. At first whichever cats I had with me would stop there, and refuse to walk past it. It was as though a signpost had been planted there saying "STOP! NO ENTRY FOR CATS!"

After a few weeks I found I could coax them past the gap but they were uneasy all the time they were in its vicinity. Then one afternoon, having my tea on the terrace, Tyfoon sitting on the wall beside me, both of us minding our own business and admiring the view, I saw the red glint of a fox's fur coming through the gap in the hedge. The fox began to trot purposefully across the field, following the little path it had obviously made over the months. Tyfoon saw it and froze. Then the fox paused and looked at Tyfoon, something threatening and menacing in the way it took in the scene.

I could do threatening and menacing too. I stood up and placed myself alongside Tyfoon, trying to convey the message, that she had reinforcements. The fox stared for another moment, then moved on. I don't suppose he gave up using what was obviously his most convenient route from his lair to the nearest source of food, but I only ever saw him once again, a couple of months later. He had been shot and was hanging in a tree near to the neighbouring farm. It could have been any old fox, I knew, but it seemed too much of a co-incidence that I never saw a fox using that path again after seeing the corpse in the tree, and the cats stopped worrying about crossing the gap in the hedge.

I had no doubt that there must have been other foxes around in that very rural landscape, and that they constituted a danger for the cats. Someone told me that a fox would be unlikely to attack a cat for fear of the damage that its claws could cause. But clearly the fox that saw Tyfoon thought about it, and just as clearly the cats were aware that fox scent equalled danger before they had even seen the fox.

To this day I still wonder how they knew. It had nothing to do with relative size, because on the afternoon when Tyfoon made the acquaintance of the herd of cows that grazed in the field alongside our garden there was no sign of animosity even though a cow is considerably larger than a cat, a fact that seemed to have escaped Tyfoon's attention until that day. She was ambling along the top of the wall, glancing curiously at the pair of cows with their heads down who were grazing along the bottom of the wall. Suddenly one of the cows raised its head and blew down its nostrils at Tyfoon, while the other approached and reached out its tongue to lick her back. A horrified Tyfoon moved very quickly out of their way and continued to watch them from a safe distance, but she wasn't frightened. She was simply annoyed at having her dignity undermined.

The other significant conflict with the local wildlife was with the rabbit population. The banks at the bases of the hedgerows that surrounded us on every side were riddled with burrows. In the mornings and evenings their occupants used to come out in family groups to graze. Tyfoon would sit and watch them, deeply interested, though I don't think they were the first rabbits she had seen – there must have been a lot of them at Can Vidal. Blackie certainly knew what they were for, and how to catch them. As soon as the baby rabbits born the next spring were large enough to pop out of their holes, Blackie would appear each morning with one of them in his mouth and sit in the middle of the lawn, where nobody could sneak up on him without being seen, and enjoy his breakfast. I think he had earmarked a couple of nearby burrows and just sat outside and waited for the babies to stick their heads out and innocently survey the world. He certainly never went without his favourite breakfast during the early summer. Fortunately for the rabbits, he was the only one who liked rabbit meat enough to take the trouble to catch them. Tyfoon, Selly and Tabitha were far too sensible to waste energy that could be devoted to lying in the sun and ambushing the neighbours' cat when she tried to cross the garden they had now claimed as their own.

As that first year in Cornwall drew to a close I was busy with a part-time job in the nearby town, and with renovating the bungalow. From the way the cats had settled in it seemed as though I had picked a perfect spot – a little bit of cat heaven. I was sure that if I could have asked them, they would have said yes, the struggle to get there had all been worth while. Even in non-cat terms, it was pretty good. I could sit on my terrace, or stand in my kitchen looking out of the window, and see the moors and beacons of Cornwall stretching away to the sea on the opposite coast. I was only sorry that David wasn't there to enjoy it with me. It was just the kind of place where he would have been happy. But even the pain of losing him was beginning to recede now that I was, for the first time since his death, living in my own place, somewhere we had never shared.

It all felt so good, as though life was once again going somewhere meaningful. I might have known it wouldn't last.

10. PARADISE LOST

"There's a beautiful black cat lying dead in the lane. Is it one of yours?"

I was working away from home that weekend, and my son was staying in the bungalow, looking after the cats. It was he who answered the door to my neighbour early on that autumn morning and he who went out and picked up Blackie from where he had landed when the passing farm van broke his neck as it came too fast around the corner in the lane.

It was so unfair!

A little country lane, perhaps one vehicle going past every couple of hours. I had thought it would be so safe for the cats. As indeed it had been up to then. By that time Blackie had enjoyed more than two years of being free to wander over the fields hunting his rabbits, of having a warm fireside on winter evenings. Then on his way home for breakfast one day he made one error of judgement as he jumped down from the hedge to cross the lane, and that was the end. The end of a brave, beautiful soul who had survived so much, snuffed out by a stupid driver who must have known he had hit an animal but hadn't even bothered to stop and check it out.

When I came home that evening I had a little

weep over him and then we buried him under a stone slab in the garden. By the next morning my grief had mutated into the kind of anger that needs to take action. I pulled some sheets of hardboard and tins of paint out of the shed and made a huge notice that I stuck on some posts in the hedge. It read:

SLOW DOWN!!   ONE OF YOU IDIOTS KILLED MY CAT ON SATURDAY AND DIDN'T EVEN BOTHER TO STOP!

I don't suppose it meant much to any passing motorist or van driver. After all, this was the countryside and country people don't bother themselves too much about the fate of animals. It made me feel better to be shouting at them all. But of course, it didn't bring Blackie back.

I made a serious mistake then. Thinking in terms of filling the gap left by Blackie's death I visited the local RSPCA Rescue Centre to look for another male cat. I made friends with a large, middle aged Persian-style tabby called Malcom who strongly resembled a stray, war-orphaned cat my sister and I had been allowed to adopt when we were children.

Malcom was only too pleased to be invited to Burngullow, especially when he realised he would be part of a gang – moreover, being the only male, he assumed he was expected to be in charge of that gang. He was scrupulously polite, careful to always do the right thing. But once he had sussed out what was the order of the day and spent a few moments watching what the other cats were doing, he would push himself to the fore and take pride of place, as though saying, No, you silly girls, this is how we'll do it. He pushed his way in front of the fire, grabbed the best spot on the bed in the evenings, jumped to the front of the food queue, and howled in fury if I tried to shut him in a separate room so that the others could have some peace.

I'm sure he would have settled down but I fear that he might never have been accepted by the girls. They just weren't ready to have a strange male cat lording it over them. For another couple of days I persisted in my efforts to persuade them to settle down and accept Malcom but when I saw that Tyfoon had moved into the shed, and Tabitha was sitting in the garden in the rain, staring with tragic eyes at the house as though she intended to leave if things didn't improve rapidly, I came to the heart-rending decision that Malcom would have to go. They were none too pleased to see him at the Rescue Centre and tried to persuade me to take him back, assuring me that he would settle down. But I couldn't risk that settling down process driving any of my gang away from the home I had made for them. For some reason that I didn't understand but that was clear to them, Malcom just didn't fit in.

My sister suggested that it was because he didn't speak Spanish.

In the end they chose Blackie's replacement themselves, and language didn't seem to be a barrier to that relationship.

Ever since I had come to Burngullow the resident cat population had been temporarily enlarged by a succession of ginger and white visitors. They usually appeared around mealtimes, though when the weather was inclement I would sometimes stroll into the kitchen in the morning to find a couple of them curled up in the radiator bed while Tyfoon and Selly looked on, disgruntled.

None of them ever stayed long and I guessed there must be a tribe of them living in a semi-neglected state on one of the neighbouring farms. One of the earliest of these visitors was nicknamed The Brigadier in honour of the crisp ginger moustache he sported in an otherwise all white face. He distinguished himself by holding the record for snaffling the top off a pizza. It was a tuna pizza and therefore doubly tempting, and the whole incident was my fault because I should have known better than to leave it cooling for a few minutes on the kitchen worktop while I went to the bathroom. I thought it would be all right because there were no cats around – mine had already had their supper. Coming back into the kitchen I was startled by a flash of ginger and white fur as The Brigadier made his exit through an open window. All that remained of the pizza was the crust base. In the few minutes I had been absent The Brig had located the source of the delicious smell and had managed to hoover every bit of the tuna, cheese and tomato topping into his hungry stomach.

The Brig disappeared during the following winter and in the spring his place was taken by a young ginger and white shorthair tom that we called Charlie.

Charlie was a fighting machine. He first came to our attention by dragging himself through our catflap, bleeding profusely from a nasty wound on his face. The fact that he had voluntarily sought me out to help him made me feel obliged to put him into a carrying box and whisk him down to the vet who cleaned the wound and gave him a shot of antibiotics and suggested that he would never keep out of fights unless I had him neutered. I explained that he wasn't really mine but the vet seemed to know about the ginger strays in that area and said she didn't think anyone would mind if I took responsibility for him.

"He's very sweet," she said. "He's got a lovely little face. But you'll never tame him while he's entire."

Charlie proved her right. Every time I made an appointment for his operation at the vet, he came in dragging some wounded limb or another, looking very sorry for himself. It was the vet who finally lost patience and took matters into her own hands by refusing to let me take Charlie home after she had dressed one set of wounds. Holding him tight, she said, "I'll keep him here until he's well enough to take the anaesthetic. I'll phone you when I've finished with him."

The cat that was returned to me after the operation was certainly quieter and more ready to become domesticated. In fact, he turned into a fine little fellow, happy to live in contented friendship with Tyfoon, Tabitha and Selly. When my son taught him to play by rolling ping-pong balls up and down the corridor, his face was a picture of delight as he suddenly realised what the point of the game was. Keen to do the right thing and be accepted, he observed how the resident cats used the litter tray, and tried to copy them, getting it slightly wrong by sitting with his rear end in the tray and his front end on the floor. "Lucky he's got the business end over the tray," observed one of my friends, watching this extraordinary performance.

Another thing Charlie loved to do was to sit partially on my lap, partially on my office table, with his chin resting on my laptop computer. At first I wondered why he did this but I realised that he was getting a small buzz of vibration from the computer. As you can imagine, this addiction caused me some inconvenience when I was working so I had to find some way of going to work in my office (which was at the bottom of the garden) without him knowing.

This was far from easy. Charlie was a bright little button and he soon cottoned on to which times of day I usually headed down to the office. He also learned the sound of the office key being lifted off the key rack by the back door. However quietly I tried to do it, the click of metal against metal brought him running, tail in the air, eager to begin the day's work.

A year later, almost to the day, Charlie made the same mistake as Blackie. He ran across the lane in front of a farm van that was being driven too fast, and it broke his neck. I was brought out into the garden by my neighbour shouting at the van, but the driver didn't stop. This time I was able to hold Charlie in my arms as the light faded from his eyes and he became one more little corpse that nobody cared about except me.

The next one to go was Tabitha, and I never even found out what happened to her. It was a bright day in October that I arrived home in the early afternoon from my part-time job in the nearby town. As soon as I got out of the car I became aware of an atmosphere of dread and shock hanging over the place, despite the sunshine.

I saw that the farm workers had been busy harvesting a field of sweetcorn alongside my bungalow, leaving the place a devastated landscape of ripped and broken corn stalks. I knew that their harvesting machine was noisy and its vibrations could be terrifying, so I was immediately concerned for the cats. When they heard me calling, Tyfoon and Selly came out from hiding places in the sheds and greenhouses, but not Tabitha. She was never seen again.

I knew that if she had been sufficiently frightened by the machinery she might simply have taken off into the surrounding fields, and I searched every inch of the adjoining hedges that afternoon, accompanied by a concerned Tyfoon who followed me everywhere a few steps behind. I found shotgun cartridges, which told me the farm workers had been shooting rabbits as they worked – might they have shot a little grey-brown cat by mistake? I noticed that on my terrace there was a drying pool of water – where had it come from on a sunny October day? Had someone climbed over my wall and used my hosepipe to wash something off the terrace that they didn't want me to find? If so, what?

My neighbour watched my search and cryptically said, "They'm afraid of you, Missus."

"Who is?"

"They contractors. They'm afraid you'll sue them."

"Why should I sue them?"

"You better ask them that." He shook his head and turned away, and nothing I could say then or later drew any more information out of him. I went to see the farmer, whose attitude was, "Oh, only a cat? What do you expect me to do?"

Well, I expected him to get up off his backside in front of the TV and at least talk to me about it, or telephone the agricultural contractors who had been working on his land (and on mine?) that morning. But he didn't even come to the front door, just conversed with me via one of his children.

So I went home and telephoned the contractors myself but they closed ranks and denied seeing a cat either in the field or in my garden.

Yet – something dreadful had happened. I felt this ugly creeping sensation that everyone knew what except for me. And perhaps Tyfoon and Selly. Something had disturbed them, for they were unduly subdued that evening. But of course they couldn't tell me.

For some reason Tabitha's disappearance affected me more than any of the other deaths and disappearances. I began to have flashbacks to David's death, which I thought I had got over, and started mourning him all over again. I began to be frightened of going out and leaving my home unattended, and when I did go out I was terrified of going home again.

My friends watched me anxiously and nodded in understanding when I said, "I can't carry on. My heart is broken."

A couple of months later I put the bungalow up for sale. I knew I had to get away from there before I lost Tyfoon and Selly as well.

11. GROWING OLD TOGETHER

I felt awful about disrupting the cats again when they had settled so well in what I had thought was the perfect environment for them. I know I hadn't actually promised them we were settled for life, but I'd sort of assumed it. Then I remembered that Tyfoon wasn't a cat who expected a settled life. She had been brought up to believe that every few days we would move our house to new surroundings which she would have the excitement of exploring. Poor Tyfoon! How bored she must have been living in the same spot for the past five years!

Anyway, I'd had enough of the country so we moved to a nice terrace house in town. It had a walled garden that I made cat-friendly with climbing areas and a hole in the wall in place of the usual cat flap so that they could come and go as they pleased. To make sure they didn't get lost or confused, they spent the two days of the move in the local cattery so that when I collected them, most of our familiar furniture was already in their new home.

When I brought them back from the cattery my theory about Tyfoon missing the stimulation of regular moving was fully vindicated. In fact both of them were pretty excited about the new place. I couldn't hear what they said to each other about it but I could tell they were happy by the way they explored, running in and out of each room in turn, together but slightly apart, as though acknowledging that although they didn't actually like each other any better than before, they appreciated the back-up for the moment.

Knowing that neither of them had ever experienced a house with an upstairs before, I wondered what they would make of the arrangement. It was fascinating to watch. After a few circuits of the downstairs rooms, getting their bearings, Tyfoon unerringly set off up the stairs (perhaps remembering a ladder in a long-ago boatyard) and they explored the upstairs rooms as well. By coffee time they knew exactly where they were, where I was and where everything they needed could be located. It took them another half a day to construct a conceptual map of where the central heating pipes passed beneath floor boards, and where the back and front windows were located in relation to each other – not easy in a house that was half way along a terrace.

After that they each chose a place to sleep and left the rest to me.

This new home was far removed from the cat heaven I had chosen at Burngullow. It had no view, no large garden, no fields full of rabbits and cows, no visiting farm cats. But there was something altogether happier about it, and once I knew that Tyfoon and Selly felt the same as I did, we settled down to a routine that served us well for several years to come. Both cats were in good health and neither seemed to mind that I had to leave them in the care of a visiting sitter (usually my son) when I had to work away from home.

But, inexorably, something I hadn't allowed for was creeping up on us.

I never gave much thought to the process of growing old while it was happening to me. I was aware of birthdays passing, of annual reminders about booster vaccinations arriving from the vet, of the onset of minor ill-health, of discussions with work colleagues about collecting our pensions, but I never looked in the mirror and thought, "Oh, that's me. Don't I look old?" Friends and family all changed so slowly that I simply didn't notice them becoming different.

And for a long while it was the same with Tyfoon and Selly. Okay, so Tyfoon tended to put on weight and had to be fed on diet biscuits about once a year. And the black part of Selly's coat began to take on that dark brown sheen, as happens to all black cats when they get older. But they were well and active – they even found their way to the allotments at the end of the lane on fine summer mornings. Their age simply didn't register as being significant until one day when I took them to the vet for their annual booster.

I was sitting in the waiting room and my eye fell on one of those posters the nurses pin up sometimes when they get bored, this one about health and relative ages of dogs and cats. According to the chart for cats, at age sixteen human years they are about the equivalent of seventy-eight years old, relative to a cat's life span.

I thought, When I am seventy-eight I shall regard myself as an old lady.

But the big point that registered was that Tyfoon had been born sixteen years before, in 1991. I knew that for certain because she was a kitten when she had been rescued by the Belgians in the little red boat. That was years ago but I still regarded her as being a young cat. I had always thought of Selly, too, as being around the same age as Tyfoon when she came to us at Can Vidal. Sixteen years ago. Really? But seventy-eight? Surely they weren't that old?

What shocked me most, as I sat there in the waiting room doing my arithmetic, was that, without my noticing, sixteen years had slipped by since we adopted Tyfoon, fifteen years since we lived on *Nyala*, fourteen since David died. And for all that time I had been arranging my life to look after Tyfoon and her friends. All that time tied up simply because one sunny morning we had casually agreed to look after one little starving stray kitten.

Where would it all end? How long would they live? How long would we all live?

Okay, so the cats were ageing more quickly relative to me. They had already overtaken me by almost one and a half theoretical decades, but it wasn't going to end there, was it? I now had responsibility for two geriatric cats, and suddenly I didn't feel all that young myself.

Not long after that epiphany we had to make another house move. My health was deteriorating and I needed to move into a bungalow or ground floor apartment while I still could. This time the move didn't go so smoothly.

As before, I sent Tyfoon and Selly to the cattery for a couple of nights in case they were upset by the packing and shifting of furniture. Within twenty-four hours of coming to her new home, Tyfoon was showing all the symptoms of cat flu. I couldn't understand why this should have happened – she had been regularly vaccinated against the virus ever since she was a kitten. The vet told me that sometimes cats came in contact with cat flu early in their lives and harboured the virus in their system for years before it broke out in a mild form. Nobody had ever told me about this. Then I remembered Ginger at Can Vidal, snuffling and coughing. Perhaps she had caught it from him, but it seemed wrong that

Tyfoon's vaccinations had been only partially effective, and even more wrong that nobody had ever warned me that this could be the case. On the other hand, Selly's vaccinations must have worked perfectly because she showed no sign of catching the flu from Tyfoon.

As I nursed Tyfoon, watching her struggling with the effects of the virus, almost unable to breathe or lap water, I was quite sure I was going to lose her. After all, she was now an old cat and old cats don't have the same reserves of stamina as when they are young. But this was Tyfoon I was dealing with, the same cat I had sat with all night as she struggled against the effects of poison long ago in a Spanish boatyard. I remembered the steely determination with which she had fought then, and I believed she was fighting just as hard now. Once again she clearly wasn't ready to go.

She tucked herself up in one of her favourite beds and raised no objection when I gave her hourly medication. She seemed to know that I desperately wanted her to be with me a little longer. To my enormous relief she gradually improved and stopped wheezing and sneezing. It was still winter and for years she had been liable to depression during the winter months. But soon she would have warm spring sunshine to speed her recovery. We relaxed and began to settle into the new home.

Sadly, while I was giving all this attention to Tyfoon I didn't notice what was happening to Selly. I did notice that she was beginning to wowl and cry more than usual but I had been told by the vet that this was normal for older cats.

"Why?" I wanted to know.

"It's a sign that they're getting confused. Maybe trying to communicate better with you."

I had the feeling that he didn't really know. I also

had the feeling that Selly wasn't settling into her new surroundings as well as I expected.

Then one evening I watched her weaving her way along the corridor that led to the kitchen and their feeding bowls. Tyfoon was sitting half way along the corridor and Selly walked straight into her, to the embarrassment and consternation of both of them. I suddenly realised - the poor darling was going blind. No wonder she had been crying and confused as she tried to get used to a strange home. Worse still, when I lifted her onto my knee and began to stroke her, I saw that she had a lump growing through the front of her skull.

The vet agreed with me that it was probably a tumour. She explained what I already knew in my heart, that she could take an x-ray but that she was unlikely to recommend operating so close to the eyes and brain, specially on such a old cat. I understood what she was trying to tell me and I already knew that Selly's suffering was only just beginning. It was time to let her go.

My son was with me, and he agreed with my decision to let the vet put her to sleep. She didn't resist as we both cuddled her while the vet clipped a patch of hair from her paw, but then she had always been a complaisant little animal. Within seconds of the needle being slipped under her skin she had gone

"Did we do the right thing?" I asked my son.

He nodded. "Couldn't you see how thin and tired she was getting? She had a lovely last day. She had a bowl of her favourite meat and gravy, she had a sleep in the sun, and lots of cuddles."

I think that was the most important thing – a lovely last day, with nothing to be frightened of. But how I missed her as I contemplated being a one-cat family again.

I would like to relate that after that Tyfoon was

able to settle down to a peaceful old age but unfortunately that wasn't the end of her traumas. A few weeks after she had recovered from the cat flu, while she was still trying to work out what had happened to her house-mate Selly, I went to London for a day to attend a meeting and while crossing the concourse at Victoria Station I fell heavily and broke my hip. I managed to hobble home, thinking at the time that I had only bruised myself, but within a few days the pain forced me to report to our local casualty department from where I was swiftly admitted to an orthopaedic ward for an operation.

Of course, Tyfoon wasn't neglected during that time. My son went to my place twice a day to feed her and play with her – he was the only male person apart from David that Tyfoon had ever accepted. But his time was limited because he was also trying to do his job and running around looking after my needs. Tyfoon must have been very sad and lonely during those weeks and must have wondered why I had suddenly deserted her, left her to look after herself, just as David had done years before at Can Vidal.

One afternoon my son rang me from my home phone to my patients' phone in the hospital. As always I was delighted to hear his voice. "Everything all right there?"

"Yes. I just thought you'd like a word with Tyfoon."

What a good idea! "Is she there?"

"Yes, sitting on my lap. I've put the receiver up to her ear. You can talk to her now."

But of course that was just what I couldn't do. I could make noises but I couldn't talk to her because I had always been too busy to learn cat. However, I did my best and we had a conversation that went something like this:

"Hello. Hello, darling."

"Awouw."

"Miaouw. Miaouw. Miaouw?"

"Miaouw, prr, prrr, prrrrr."

"Hello?"

"Awouw."

It went on like that for a few expensive minutes, encouraged by my son who said, "She's definitely listening to you."

Conversation finished, I hung up the phone and glanced around the ward. I suddenly realised that I wasn't alone and that the nurses, and the ladies in the beds on either side of me, were looking at me a little strangely.

"Who were you talking to?" one of them ventured. I wondered if they had ever before heard anyone have a full-fledged telephone conversation in miaouws.

I said, as casually as I could, "Oh, that was my little cat asking when I'm coming home."

"Could she hear you?"

"Yes, of course."

"And could she understand what you were saying?"

"I think so. Otherwise why would she have replied?"

They shook their heads in amazement and obviously thought that I was more than a little crazy.

I tried to explain that Tyfoon always greeted me by saying "Awouw", her version of "Hello". I'm quite sure that in her mind the vocabulary of squeaks and wowls she developed over the years was a perfectly comprehensible translation of the noises I made at her. She long ago decided that if I couldn't speak cat she was going to do her best to speak person.

These days she can make it perfectly clear to me

that she is hungry, she wants the radiators turned up, she wants the gas fire turned on, she wants to go into the garden, it's getting cold and she wants to get under the duvet with me, she's feeling insecure and will I please not go out and leave her on her own.

As for the vet's idea that she's losing her marbles as she grows older...nah.   It's me that's losing my marbles. Tyfoon is just finding cleverer ways of keeping me in line as I grow older and more confused.

11. DREAMTIME

Which of us was more pleased to see the other when, after two and a half dreadful weeks, I was allowed home from hospital? Tyfoon expressed her feelings by not allowing me out of her sight, day or night. That caused no problems at first because I was unable to go anywhere. I couldn't drive and I was frightened of venturing outside on my crutches in case I fell again. For a few weeks everyone I needed came to see me, though I knew that before long I was going to have to pull myself together and get organised, at least to hobble to the nearest shop.

If I hadn't had Tyfoon to consider, that pulling together would have taken a very long time. As it was, she needed to be fed, preferably on the boiled white fish that had been her favourite ever since the days when we fished for mullet off the boat. In addition, her litter tray needed daily attention, she wanted to sit outside in the courtyard garden and soak up the sun, and she wanted to be with me.

Her needs wrapped themselves around my existence and I found myself planning my days to suit her. All this focus on my cat may seem like spoiling her, but it was more important than that. My doctor explained what happened to a lot of people with orthopaedic problems. "They come home from hospital, arrange their armchair where it's warm and the remote where they can reach it and never move again."

Tyfoon's presence made certain that couldn't happen to me. Because I had her to look after, I *had* to get up in the morning, however much of a struggle it was. I *had* to move around, I *had* to think of someone other than myself.

The plain fact was that without Tyfoon I might never have become fully mobile again. With her, life had some sort of structure however ragged it turned out some days.

I knew that together we were settling into the roles of eccentric old lady and demanding old cat and I supposed that the rest of the world must have smiled indulgently whenever they caught sight of us together. But I didn't care and nor did Tyfoon.

My health is better now. I can drive my car, walk without a stick, go pretty well anywhere I want to. But I wonder about Tyfoon. This spring her age is creeping up to eighty-six years old, she is arthritic and grumpy, needing medication every day to overcome the pain in her limbs. I have a little while to go before I'm eighty-six but I notice that Tyfoon spends most of her time sleeping. I take that as a hint for my own future – but not yet.

We live less than a hundred yards from the sea, and the channel where fishing boats make their way in and out of the harbour runs close to the back of our apartment. Though Tyfoon can't see the water, when I open the windows in the morning she sits and sniffs the air in just the same way as she used to sniff out the fish markets when we sailed into foreign ports. So she knows we are living in a proper place for sea-going cats and people, even if she can't actually make another voyage.

I would take her if I thought she wanted to go, but these days she is no longer the confident captain of a cat that she used to be. She will rarely come out into the front garden with me and when she does, the sight and sound of a motor vehicle sends her scuttling back indoors. I think she has had enough of adventures. I can understand that.

Often when she wakes up she calls out in a panic because she doesn't know where I am, and I worry that she shouldn't be so dependent on me because, after all, I might go first. But then I watch her curled up in the sun or beside a radiator and I know she hasn't much time left. One day she will go to sleep and simply not wake up. The vet says she is very healthy for her age and she has years to go yet. But some days I see that distant, far away look in her yellow eyes and I know that already she's not really with me.

I wonder what she dreams about. There must be dreams for all those hours she spends asleep. Sometimes her legs and her whiskers twitch and I can see her creeping through the undergrowth, stalking some interesting insect to bring us as a gift. Sometimes when she wakes with a start and a cry, I know she's been somewhere else, perhaps preparing for a fight or taking a ducking. Compared to the average cat who rarely changes its environment, there are so many places for her memories to take her. Is her little brain sufficiently well wired to recall them all?

I wonder, does she dream about the warmth of her mother's milk, her tiny paws kneading the teat to fill her mouth? Does she dream of the workmen shouting, of the fear and the fire, of being left alone in the darkness, cold and searching for her lost mother?

Or does she have happy dreams of games with a nice man who was never too tired to throw a ball for her to catch? Of the wind ruffling her fur, and rigging to climb? Of buckets of sand to be scattered to the four winds? Of fish markets and bushes to be explored in strange towns? Of strange insects? Of a Spanish hillside where she learned to hunt with other cats? Of the fields of Burngullow and the farm cats that used to call by and borrow her radiator bed?

Does she sometimes wake with a start at the sound of an engine, imagining she is still in the hold of the aeroplane, terrified, not knowing what is going to happen to her next?

And does she dream about the cats who have walked beside her – Peanut, Hourigan, Big Ginger's family, Blackie, Tabitha, Charlie, Selly – all gone ahead of her now?

One thing is certain. I will never forget her. And when she goes into that final, deep sleep and doesn't come back, she will take part of me with her.

BY THE SAME AUTHOR

<u>NOVELS</u>

THE COMPLETE KNOWLEDGE OF SALLY FRY
(Gollancz 1983)

What is to be done when your son has run away from
home and even retreating to a remote holiday cottage
in Cornwall with a mother who is adept at attracting
problems has not brought the required peace and
quiet? For harassed heroine Sally Fry the answer is
to write her Complete Knowledge, which she hopes
will make sense of her haphazard life.
A novel of exceptional panache – TheLiterary Review

THE LIFE AND TIMES OF BARLY BEACH
(Gollancz 1987)

The little fishing village of Barly provides an ideal refuge for recently divorced city girl, Jenny Sharpe, and
her young son Thomas. Over the years Barly comes
under threat both from the encroaching suburbs of the
neighbouring seaside resort but also from the greedy
property developers who have been secretly buying
up land in and around the village.
Splendid, unpretentious comedy –The Times
Lucid and witty – Daily Telegraph

CANDY'S CHILDREN

w(Greenland 2007)
A wealthy Palestinian businessman, a middle-aged rock star, an Australian university lecturer, a nun and an English aristocrat – why are these five ill-assorted people meeting up in a stately home in Yorkshire? They are the children of candy Price, one-time film star and recently dowager countess of Penmore. She has been murdered by an assassin's bomb on a mysterious visit to Tel Aviv and they are gathering for her funeral – an event that will change all their lives one way or another.
Superior saga - Nicholas Clee, The Guardian Review
A gripping novel – Western Morning News

CROCODILES

(Legend Press – 2008)
After the collapse of his comfortable life as an up-an-coming city banker Paul Tolley answers a cry for help from Africa where his brother Rob, who runs a tourist lodge, has disappeared. Paul knows nothing about Africa and soon learns that nothing is what it seems and nobody can be trusted. Everything is dangerous, the people as well as the wildlife, and in particular the crocodiles among them who are ready to devour anything in their path.

SELF-HELP

DEALING WITH A DEATH IN THE FAMILY

(How to Books – 1997)
How to manage the emotional and practical difficulties surrounding a death. Much as we may prefer to avoid thinking about it, sooner of later every family has to face up to the death of one of its members. This book is a must for everyone who has to work their way through the practical maze of legal and social arrangements which must be completed before they can be left in peace to mourn.

SURVIVING YOUR PARTNER

(How to Books – 1998
2nd edition – Greenland – 2005)
Living with the death of the person closest to you. Losing your life's partner is a devastating experience. Not only is there bereavement and all its associated problems to face, there is also the prospect of becoming single again. This book addresses and analyses those problems and provides strategies to help the survivor to move on in a life that must, of necessity, be changed for ever.
This book gives the bereaved hope and empowerment – George Penaluna – The Friend

BOATBUILDING

KEEPING NYALA IN STYLE

(Waterline – 1995)
Improving a classic boat and maintaining her original elegance. The story of how the author and her husband brought the boat up to a suitable standard for long-term cruising. As the story unfolds, each step of the work is carefully explained and beautifully illustrated. Sylvia has written and illustrated numerous articles for the yachting press and this book is used as a reference book by many owners of wooden boats.